JOHN PAUL THE GREAT

MAKER OF THE POST-CONCILIAR CHURCH

John Paul the Great

Maker of the Post-Conciliar Church

IGNATIUS PRESS   SAN FRANCISCO

Printed in 2005 by Ignatius Press, San Francisco.
Printed in the United States of America ∞

First printed by the Catholic Truth Society, London, 2003
© *2003 by the Catholic Herald & the Catholic Truth Society*

All rights reserved. Published 2003 by The Incorporated Catholic Truth Society 40-46 Harleyford Road London SE11 5AY & The Catholic Herald, Lamb's Passage, Bunhill Row, London EC1Y 8TQ

ISBN   1-58617-112-7

Front cover image: *Pope John Paul II closes the holy door of Saint Peter's Basilica on Saturday, 6th January 2001.* Courtesy of PA Photos, London. Inside images courtesy of L'Osservatore Romano, PA News and The Catholic Herald.

Contents

Contributors

Tracey Rowland is the Dean of the John Paul II Institute for Marriage and Family (Melbourne) and a Permanent Fellow of the Institute in Political Philosophy and Continental Theology. She holds degrees in law, politics and philosophy from the Universities of Queensland and Melbourne and a doctorate from the Divinity School of the University of Cambridge. She is the author of *Culture and the Thomist Tradition: after Vatican II* (Routledge: London, 2003). Her major field of research is the development of a theology of culture.

Ian Ker is a parish priest and tutor at Campion Hall, Oxford, where he is a member of the theology faculty. He has taught English and theology in universities in Britain and the United States. He is the author and editor of twenty books on Newman, including *John Henry Newman: A Biography* (1988). His new book *The Catholic Revival in English Literature, 1845-1966* will be published shortly. In 2001 the Catholic Truth Society published his *The New Movements: A Theological Introduction*.

Agneta Sutton, who wrote her Ph.D on John Paul II's sexual ethics at King's College, University of London, is Associate Lecturer in Moral Theology at University College Chichester and Head of Research at the London-based Centre for Bioethics and Public Policy Chichester. She also lectures in moral theology at Heythrop College, University of London and has a regular column in the *Catholic Times*. She is married with four grown-up children.

William Oddie is editor of the *The Catholic Herald*; his books include: *What will happen to God?* and the *Roman Option*. He was ordained an Anglican clergyman in 1977; in 1991 he was received into the Catholic Church.

John Saward is Senior Professor at the International Theological Institute in Gaming, Austria. He is the author of six books, including: *Christ is the Answer: The Christ-Centred Teaching of Pope John Paul II*. He is also a visiting professor at the Newman Institute in Ballina, Ireland, and at the John Paul II Institute in Melbourne, Australia.

Brendan Leahy is a lecturer in theology at the Mater Dei Institute of Education, a college of Dublin City University. A priest of the Dublin Archdiocese, he is Secretary of the Irish Bishops' Advisory Committee on Ecumenism. In addition to his other publications, he is the author of *The Marian Profile in the Ecclesiology of Hans Urs von Balthasar* (London: New City, 2000).

Aidan Nichols, OP, an English Dominican, is authour of some thirty books on different aspects of historical and dogmatic theology. He is currently the priar of Blackfriars Cambridge.

Rodger Charles SJ is a moral and pastoral theologian and member of the University of Oxford Theology faculty and has been researching, writing and lecturing on Catholic social teaching for over thirty years. His main publications on the subject are *The Social Teaching of Vatican II* (1982), the two volume *Christian Social Witness and Teaching: the Catholic Tradition from Genesis to Centesimus Annus* (1998) and the short *Introduction to Catholic Social Teaching* (1999).

Léonie Caldecott is a writer specialising in religious and cultural issues. With her husband Stratford she edits the journal *Second Spring*, published by the Chesterton Institute for Faith and Culture in Oxford. She is also a regular contributor to the *Chesterton Review* and the *Catholic Herald*, as well as a number of other publications. In 1995 she founded the Rose Round, an initiative for girls, which organises cultural events, retreats and pilgrimages, and which sprang directly from her experience as a mother of three daughters, now in their teens.

Acknowledgements

The origins of this book are in a one-day conference on the achievements of the present pontificate, organised in Oxford in 2001 by the Chesterton Institute for Faith and Culture. My first acknowledgment, therefore, must be to the Institute's director, Stratford Caldecott, for inviting me to open the conference: I did so with a paper entitled John Paul the Great, a revised version of which forms my opening chapter. My grateful thanks are due also to Angela and Armand de Malherbe, in whose house in the Loire I wrote it. Earlier versions of two other chapters, those of John Saward and Rodger Charles SJ, were delivered at the same conference. My thanks are due to all the contributors, but particularly to Fr Ian Ker, for many discussions on and around issues addressed in these pages. This book is the first joint publication by The Catholic Herald and the Catholic Truth Society. I am grateful to Ignatius Kusiak, publisher of the Herald and Fergal Martin, General Secretary of the CTS, for their enthusiasm for the project, and to Piero Finaldi of the CTS for his help with several editorial difficulties, not least the alarming discovery, as my final deadline approached, that the final edited versions of all the chapters proved to have been infected by a mysterious virus (by which I had already paralysed the computer of one contributor), a problem with which he coped with reassuring sang froid.

William Oddie
8 September 2003

I

JOHN PAUL THE GREAT

William Oddie

About a decade ago, the late Professor Adrian Hastings - having the previous year published his controversial though unsurprising book *The Theology of a Protestant Catholic* - edited a substantial volume entitled *Modern Catholicism, Vatican II and After*. It was a collection of essays containing contributions from what the dust jacket described as 'an international team of leading Catholic scholars'; and among these contributions was an assessment of the pontificate thus far of the Pope from Poland, by the distinguished commentator on Vatican affairs, the late Peter Hebblethwaite. It concluded with these words:

> One would like to think that John Paul continues to learn from his stay in the West, not to mention his world-wide journeys; and that he might spend as much time trying to understand the rest of us as we have spent trying to understand him. It may be that his providential role is to test the conservative hypothesis to breaking point. At the conclave that elected him, it was possible to argue that the Church needed a strong hand on the tiller. At the next conclave, that argument will not wash: the

conservative option will have been tried, and may well be found wanting. In the spiritual life, everyone fails. The seed falls into the ground and dies. But this will be a magnificent heroic failure on a cosmic scale, with that special Polish dash.

A year or two later, in a little restaurant close to St Peter's, the same writer was quoted in the *Catholic World Report* as saying that 'Nothing he has done will outlast him. Not the *Catechism*, not *Veritatis splendor*, not the document on the ordination of women.... The new man will put aside everything John Paul has done and start ... again'.

I remembered these judgements in Westminster Cathedral, as I was listening, early in the new Millennium, to a lecture (sponsored by *The Catholic Herald*) given by the Pope's biographer, George Weigel. It was entitled 'The achievement of John Paul II'. It was not so much that Weigel's assessment of the Pope was very different, though certainly it was: John Paul's pontificate, he concluded, was 'the most consequential since the Protestant reformation of the sixteenth century'.

But it was the people who had come to hear Weigel speak who were as interesting as the lecture itself: apart from anything else, there were so many of them. Originally, the plan had been for the lecture to take place in a hall seating about 200 people. But it was soon clear that this would have to be rethought: the lecture was moved to the nave of the Cathedral, which holds about 1,000: and every seat was taken.

Ten years before, such a response would not have been imaginable: what was the explanation? Why had they all come? They came, perhaps, partly because Weigel was known to have had the Pope's co-operation: the people had come to hear about the Pope's achievement from someone who could be trusted not to diminish it: what the people wanted, so it seemed to me, was an authentic assessment of the man who had become - if the somewhat Blairite language may be permitted - the people's Pope. Weigel's judgment on the pontificate's historical importance would have been controversial only a few short years before. Among those gathered in Westminster Cathedral that day, it had become so obvious that its restatement by George Weigel had about it a kind of ritual formality. It may be true that the Church thinks in millennia and not in decades; but a lot can happen in ten years, nevertheless.

We need to return, all the same, to that early judgment of Peter Hebblethwaite's, and particularly to his speculation that it was the Pope's providential role to 'test the Conservative hypothesis to breaking point'. In one sense, we can say simply that this prediction has already been very comprehensively falsified. There is much less chance today of being unthinkingly labelled 'right wing' simply for accepting this Pope's teachings on faith and morals out of conviction rather than reluctant acquiescence. As for John Paul himself, far from being perceived today as a reactionary Pope who has sought to reverse the advances inaugurated by the second Vatican Council (the so-called 'restorationist' analysis or scenario) it is, on the contrary, he who in the end has been perceived as the Council's most definitive interpreter and advocate. In the words of the Jesuit theologian Cardinal Avery Dulles, 'more than any other single individual he has succeeded in comprehensively restating the contours of Catholic faith in the light of Vatican II and in relation to postconciliar developments in the Church and in the world.'

This had, of course, been his intention from the beginning: after his election, he told the assembled Cardinals that his first task and 'definitive duty' was to complete the implementation of the Second Vatican Council. But that is not, as we all know, how it was seen by some in the early years of the pontificate. The Pope's declaration was duly noted: but it soon began to cause confusion, particularly among many of those deeply devoted to a phenomenon widely known at the time as 'the spirit of Vatican II'. What could not be gainsaid by anyone was the Pope's transparently sincere enthusiasm for the Council he had attended. But it seemed clear, to some at least, that he really did not have the slightest idea what it had all been about. This conclusion was buttressed by an assumption - often quite openly expressed - that Vatican II was largely the province of the Western Catholic intelligentsia, whose understanding of the Council was necessarily deeper and more subtle than the understanding of unsophisticated Eastern European prelates like the former Archbishop of Cracow, cut off as he had been for so long from the sophisticated intellectual life enjoyed by theologians and journalists in such great Catholic centres as Tübingen and Oxford. The difficulty for some observers, in Peter Hebblethwaite's words, was that though 'utterly sincere when he declared his commitment to them, [the Pope] nevertheless does not mean by "Council" and "Vatican II" what most people in the West mean.'

But what, we have to ask, did *that* mean? What it meant, of course, was that this Pope consistently refused to accept the view that Vatican II represented a radical break with Catholic tradition. As he declared in February, 2000, 'If anyone reads the Council presuming that it marked a break with the past, while in reality it placed itself in line with the faith of all time, he definitely has gone astray'. Thus, as Tracey Roland explains (p.27, at p.31) 'Throughout the past quarter century a major aspect of his pontificate has ... been the clarification, development and implementation of the decrees of the Council in a manner which perfects rather than destroys elements of pre-Conciliar theology'. It is probably fair to say that by the end of the twentieth century the Pope's view of the Council had become the normal view of ordinary faithful Catholics, the *sensus fidelium* yet again proving a surer guide than the self-appointed *nomenklatura* of the alternative or parallel magisterium.

There is a problem, nevertheless. For, though it is a temptation, in one way, simply to say that what we might call the anti-conservative hypothesis about Pope John Paul is not in the latter part of his pontificate looking very persuasive - in the sense that it is highly unlikely that in Hebblethwaite's words 'the new man will put aside everything John Paul has done and start ...again' - there is, nevertheless, a sense in which the judgment that the Pope is an essentially conservative figure dogs him yet. It is hard for anyone, even his enemies, to say that he is not a truly remarkable man. That now goes without saying. This is a Pope of real and undeniable stature.

But what else do we need to say? How will we think of him in the decades to come? How will he be seen by the world? These are not unimportant questions: for the higher our view of his legacy, the more sure it is that his legacy will be a determining factor in how the Church continues to face the third Millennium. And the higher the view taken by the world - even when it understands him only dimly - the more it will be inclined to take seriously a Church which both produced and has in turn been so massively influenced by such a figure.

I have referred in passing to George Weigel's assessment, that John Paul's pontificate has been the most consequential since the Protestant reformation. In his biography, he based this judgment on what he considered the Pope's eight greatest achievements: by the time he gave his *Catholic Herald* lecture in Westminster Cathedral, the list had grown to ten: the renovation of the papacy, the full implementation of Vatican II, the collapse of communism, the clarification of the moral challenges facing free society, the insertion of ecumenism into the heart of Catholicism, the new dialogue with Judaism, the redefinition of inter-religious dialogue, a fresh approach to the sexual revolution with his theology of the body, the Catechism and what it represents, and the personal inspiration that has changed countless personal lives.

This is a clear and unambiguous assessment, though I think that Weigel's list of achievements is still incomplete. Most notably, it fails to register the Pope's powerful support for the new ecclesial movements, a support which, as Ian Ker says (p. 49), 'is firmly in the tradition of the popes who, at critical times in the Church's life, have discerned dramatic new ways in which the Spirit has raised up new charismatic movements for the renewal and the propagation of the Christian faith'.

But even if Weigel's assessment had given a full and complete account of the Pope's achievements, it would still be seen by many (especially among secular observers) unduly oversimplified as a representation of the pontificate. For much of the Pope's reign - certainly for the secular world but also for many Catholics - he has been a figure of paradox. He has been, so it is said, a social progressive but an ecclesiological reactionary; a pastoral bishop who had been deeply influenced by the second Vatican Council but who then - or so some critics volubly assert even now - directed his entire pontificate towards a restoration of the Catholicism of the pre-conciliar period. He was a defender of liberty wherever the rights of men and women were denied by despotic regimes; and yet, his enemies soon began to claim that he himself silenced dissent among bishops and clergy quite as ruthlessly as any secular dictator. It seemed to many that he was wholly out of touch with the secular realities amid which he lived; and yet, almost uniquely among his contemporaries, he had a profound and subtle understanding of the nature of the historical forces that were to sweep away the post-war division of Europe between the capitalist West and the communist East.

Paradoxical or not, the achievement is there; it is solid and it is undeniable. However we resolve (or preferably deny) the supposed paradoxes, the general assessment now tends to be, in A.N.Wilson's words, that he is 'unique, infinitely the most striking and interesting figure of our times'. But is there, in fact, a lot more to say: is John Paul simply a striking and interesting figure, even if he is the most striking and the most interesting of our times? Or are we talking about an historical figure whose actions and whose personal qualities have not only influenced one of the great turning points in human affairs but also inaugurated the regeneration of the Church itself? Is this one of those rare beings who possesses, truly, those qualities of vision and intensity of focus as well as of strength and originality that allow us to say, not only here is John Paul, an exceptional Pope: but also, quite simply, here, truly, is *Joannes Paulus Magnus*, John Paul the Great?

*

The problem has to do with that word 'conservative': we no longer, it seems, know what to do with it. A conservative is now seen as someone whose mind is focused simply on preserving what he has received: his gaze is averted firmly from any notion that what he has received might contain implications for the future which permit, or even demand, that there might have to be substantial change. And that, indeed, was the assumption of many who supposed themselves to be radicals, about the Pope's view of the Council. To quote Peter Hebblethwaite again, according to the Pope's understanding, 'the purpose of the Council was essentially defensive. It was a matter of warding off errors, of preserving the deposit of faith'. The trouble with such an assessment today - and had Peter Hebblethwaite lived, he might well have come to see the point (he soon amended his dismissive view of *Veritatis splendor*) - the trouble is that this really does not sound very much like the Pope we actually have: 'defensive' is not a word which readily springs to mind.

But certainly we can accept that he is a conservative: the real question is what we mean when we say that. According to John Henry Newman, in a remarkably interesting discussion of Pope Gregory the Great, popes are necessarily conservative, in the sense that 'they cannot bear anarchy, they think revolution an evil, they pray for the peace of the world'. But, continues Newman, 'a Conservative, in the political sense of the word, signifies something else, which the Pope never is, and cannot be. It means a man who is at the top of the tree, and knows it, and means never to come down, whatever it may cost him to keep his place there ... It means a man who defends religion, not for religion's sake, but for the sake of its accidents and externals; and in this sense Conservative a Pope never can be...'

But, says Newman, 'there is a more subtle form of Conservatism, by which ecclesiastical persons are more likely to be tempted and overcome.... This fault is an over-attachment to the ecclesiastical establishment, as such ... to traditional lines of policy, precedent and discipline, - to rules and customs of long standing. But a great Pontiff must be detached from everything save the deposit of faith... He may use, he may uphold, he may and will be very slow to part with, a hundred things which have grown up, or taken shelter, or are stored, under the shadow of the Church; but, at bottom, and after all he will be simply detached.' So though they are conservative, Newman says, it is not in any bad sense: for although 'the Popes have been old men', they 'have never been slow to venture out upon a new line, when it was necessary. And, thus independent of times and places, the Popes have never found any difficulty, when the proper moment came, of following out a new and daring line of policy ... of leaving the old world to shift for itself and to disappear from the scene'.

What has surely become clear beyond any doubt is that this Pope's conservatism is of the kind that Newman is describing here; that is the conservatism of which an essential element is the detachment typical of what Newman calls the Great pontiff - and he was speaking particularly of Gregory the Great - from everything save the deposit of faith.

It is surely the Pope's ability 'when the proper moment came, [to follow] out a new and daring line of policy' that has more and more formed the public perception of this Pope, a growing understanding that he is not - or at any rate not outside the pages of *The Guardian* newspaper - to be dismissed by evoking the reactionary caricature much more common in his earlier years. A.N. Wilson's assessment that the Pope is, 'unique, infinitely the most striking and interesting figure of our times' was made in the immediate aftermath of his penitential visit to Yad Vashem, Israel's holocaust memorial, a previously unimaginable event which unfolded in a year of such striking initiatives. The Pope's visible pain and frailty had given rise some months before to speculation that he might even retire: and yet, these have been precisely the years in which not only the inner strength but also the true radicalism of this wholly unpredictable figure have become most strikingly apparent.

Indeed, it becomes clear that 'conservative' is a word we have to be very careful in using to describe this Pope, unless we understand it to mean something very close to the reverse of what it is generally assumed to mean. But this should be no surprise to Catholics unless we are to deny the very essence of the Catholic faith itself, a vital part of which precisely is to refuse to allow the deposit of faith to be compromised by the intellectual fashions of the passing age. It is what we conserve that makes us radical.

Thus, for example, the 1984 apostolic exhortation *Redemptionis donum* to men and women in religious orders, urges them to wear their habits, not for tradition's sake or because the dress matters in itself: what matters as Richard John Neuhaus put it in *The Catholic Moment* 'is that the world be confronted by their consecrated lives, by the contrast between their radical devotion and the ways of the world: not to condemn the world but to call "the people of the world" to their own potential for devotion.'

The Catholic is thus essentially a sign of contradiction to the secular culture (not just this secular culture, but all secular cultures) and when he is not confronting it - when, indeed, he is affirming it on its own terms - it is he who is the reactionary because he has fatally undermined the Christian religion's essentially radical base. He has become a collaborator with a Babylonian captivity of the mind, in which the siren call to be attractive to the world by adopting its most apparently enlightened values has triumphed.

There has to be about being a Catholic - as there has to be, indeed, in any attempt at moral or intellectual integrity - a certain element of bloody-mindedness, an element of obdurate refusal to conform. That is what we need to understand by the word 'conservative', used theologically. Thus, writing as an outside observer, the Anglican Church historian, Edward Norman, characterised the documents of the Second Vatican Council as being essentially conservative, 'in the sense that the "mystery" of the Church was never submerged beneath accommodations to the values of the secular culture'.

The truly great Pope is thus one who is able to confront the world without denying it, to confront it by asserting the values of the gospel and the mystery of the Church, to affirm it by proclaiming and defending the sacredness of every human person. We need to repeat, for these are no empty words, that his denial of the world's values will never be a withdrawal from the world: the great popes have seen the signs of the times and have read them aright.

The two popes called 'the great' - that is, Leo and Gregory - both lived in times of vast geo-political upheavals in which they themselves were major players, both defending and preserving the Church herself and exercising a direct influence over the historical forces that had been unleashed by the great struggles for power that unfolded around them. Here, surely, may be discerned a clear parallel with the present Pope. An episode in the life of Leo the Great is particularly striking. In the year 452 when Northern Italy was under attack by Attila the Hun, Leo faced him near Mantua and persuaded him to withdraw his army. This episode is commemorated by a slightly absurd bas-relief in St Peter's basilica, which shows Leo in full papal rig, including the triple crown, with Attila recoiling in fear and amazement. There are differing versions of what actually happened (financial and other inducements may have played their part); but on any account, it was a triumph for Leo's powers of persuasion and for his grasp of geopolitical realities. 'I can conquer men', Attila is recorded as saying: 'but not the Lion' (Leo).

These events surely recall irresistibly an episode in the pontificate of Pope John Paul. By the beginning of

December, 1980, in response to the Polish Solidarity movement's extraordinary success, the Soviets had made a definite decision to invade Poland and moved several divisions of the Red Army up to the Polish border. Their plans were precise. After a massive two day military operation, the Solidarity leadership would be liquidated by summary courts-martial and firing squads. There would then be installed a regime of the most brutal repression. On December 16, the Pope wrote a letter to the Soviet Leader, Leonid Brezhnev. It is written in the stilted language of diplomacy: but its message is firm. It conveys clearly without actually threatening it, that this invasion would be different, that the Poles would resist. We cannot say with certainty that this letter was what persuaded the Soviets to draw back (though the Red Army was indeed withdrawn a few days later) and to adopt an entirely different strategy for Poland: but we can certainly say that the Polish problem had become intractable mainly because of the Pope's influence, that the Russians had come to understand this, and that without him, Soviet policy would have been vastly different. There could now be no more invasions.

Gregory the Great, too, was faced with a period of political instability. He took over the governance of the city of Rome, feeding a starving people; and he saw to the city's defence, raising troops and resisting a number of incursions from the North. Undoubtedly all this was part of a process leading to the growth of the secular political powers of the papacy, now, in the immortal words of *1066 and all that*, universally held to be 'a bad thing'.

And here, in a vital sense we can say that this Pope's geopolitical involvements show him to have exceeded in the worldly sense and transcended in the spiritual sense both of these two great predecessors. The collapse of the Eastern bloc is one of the great historical convulsions: this Pope not merely expected it and prayed for it, he played by general consent a large part in bringing it about. But we have to say more than that. We need to say that this vast political result was brought about, not by a reversion into the papacy's history of political intrigue and direct involvement in the deployment of worldly power, but by asserting the superior strength of the power of the spirit. The political levers of power were never directly an object of his concern: and yet those in the Solidarity movement who did confront the Polish secular state were motivated by a Catholic humanism in which the dignity of beings made in the image of God was central, and which had been powerfully revitalised by John Paul's charismatic evangelical presence.

As the Pope insisted in his first encyclical, *Redemptor hominis*, 'The Church must in no way be confused with the political community, nor bound to any political system. She is at once a sign and a safeguard of the transcendence of the human person.' The Church is, as it were, a carrier of transcendence; and so too can be a human culture that has been impregnated by the values of the gospel. Where a Christian culture is subordinated to a political culture which is radically hostile to it, then the revitalisation of that culture's deepest roots can only lead to political destabilisation and collapse, as it did in Poland. But that is not to interfere in politics; it is to do something much more radical than that: it is to assert the primacy of culture. 'How many divisions has the Pope?' Stalin once famously sneered:

this Pope demonstrated that in the end 'divisions' are not really what counts, even in the exercise of earthly power.

The other striking parallel with both Leo and Gregory has been in John Paul's ultimately successful reassertion of the authority of the pope to teach and define doctrine. Here, we have a slight difference of approach to register: at first, we might be tempted to think that John Paul is more like Leo than Gregory. Leo, of course, was the Pope who sent the Council of Chalcedon his famous tome - a statement defining the doctrine of the two natures of Christ - with the instruction that it was to be accepted by the Council without any inquiry or discussion. *Roma locuta est*; *causa finita est* is not one of Leo's sayings; but there can be little doubt that he did more than any other pope to establish what has been a central part of the papacy's functions ever since, the duty to defend the stable and objective character of Catholic teaching.

This has not always been the way in which these two popes have been assessed. As Ian Ker put it in a review for *The Catholic Herald* of the *Short History of the Catholic Church*, by that great scourge of magisterial authority, Hans Küng: 'in Küng's view Leo was the pope with whom the rot set in'. Gregory, however, was a very different kind of pope, according to Küng: so different indeed was he in the Küngian scenario, that he should be taken as a model of how the papacy ought to have developed. 'Whereas Leo the Great advocated a proud and dominating understanding of primacy,' wrote Küng, 'Gregory the Great advocated a humble and collegial one. Had the papacy of the subsequent period orientated itself more on Gregory than on Leo in its understanding of office the *ecclesia catholica* of the middle ages could have developed along the lines of the earliest Church ... with a democratic collegial constitution and with a Roman primacy of service.'

But this is surely utterly fantastical. Certainly, it is true that Gregory described himself truthfully as 'servant of the servants of God'; and certainly, he tended not to assert his own views about the primacy over all other bishops of the bishop of Rome. 'When he reproved a fellow bishop' says Professor Mayr Harting, 'he preferred to play down the papal position and rather emphasise the bond of brotherly love between them', something, we might note in passing, the present Pope has been very inclined to do with his Orthodox brethren. But there is no evidence that Gregory had anything remotely approaching modern Küngian notions of 'democratic collegiality'. It was, after all, Gregory who first used the phrase *ex cathedra* to indicate that he was speaking with the full weight and authority of the papal office.

And for a pope to use his authority for the defence of doctrine is in any case not to be proud and arrogant; it is the very essence of his servitude to the servants of God. Indeed, it can hardly be exercised at all without the most extreme humility: for in defining or articulating Catholic teaching he must himself be no more than a channel or conduit for the mind of the Church herself.

*

There may have been popes whose lives were not ones of sacrificial service to the people of God: but Leo was not one, and Gregory was not one and John Paul is not one. The older John Paul becomes, the more clear it is that here is a man who lives wholly for God and for the people of God.

The older he becomes, too, the more startlingly original he grows, the more he bears out that judgment of Newman's: that although 'the [great] Popes have been old men', they 'have ... never found any difficulty ... [in] following out a new and daring line of policy ... of leaving the old world to shift for itself and to disappear from the scene'.

It takes more than originality to be a great pope: it takes courage, the kind of courage which becomes infectious, so that it infuses the minds and hearts of the faithful. 'Be not afraid', said John Paul in his inaugural sermon as pope; it was a sermon which powerfully established not only the tone of his pontificate but the breadth of his own mind and the vast scale on which he assessed the possibilities for the Church in the modern world:

> 'Be not afraid to welcome Christ and accept his power. Help the Pope and all those who wish to serve Christ and with Christ's power to serve the human person and the whole of mankind.
>
> Be not afraid. Open wide the doors for Christ. To his saving power open the boundaries of states, economic and political systems, the vast fields of culture, civilisation and development.
>
> Be not afraid. Christ knows 'what is in man'. He alone knows it.'

Be not afraid - it has been the watchword for his papacy: not because he has obsessively repeated it for others to follow, but because he has lived it out himself. He is in constant pain; his hands shake with Parkinson's disease; and still he does not spare himself. The older and more frail he becomes, the more his courage shines out, and the nearer his papal service comes to being a kind of living martyrdom. The word 'indomitable' springs to mind; and for an Englishman of my generation that will tend to be followed by the word 'Churchillian': for surely, in the spiritual warfare of our age, he has been one of the great heroes of the faith, not merely a great warrior himself, but an inspirer in others of the virtues of courage and persistence to the end. In due course, it will be for the Church to declare if this has been the life of one of her saints: but certainly, by any human measure current among his own contemporaries, his qualities have amounted to greatness of the highest order.

It is surely hard to believe that that will not be the verdict of history, too.

II

RECLAIMING THE TRADITION: JOHN PAUL II AS THE AUTHENTIC INTERPRETER OF VATICAN II

Tracey Rowland

Vatican II was an intellectual, spiritual and cultural event in the life of the Church of such magnitude that some argue it was unprecedented, while others suggest a comparison with the Council of Jerusalem in AD49. Just as Jerusalem stands for the decision to extend the Church's mission to the Gentiles, there is a sense that Vatican II stands for a transition in the Church's understanding of her mission and the means by which to effect it. However, whereas with Jerusalem it is relatively easy to point to the defining issue of the Council, with Vatican II neither the spirit nor the doctrine was so easily pinned down in the years immediately following its conclusion. In the 1960's and 1970's the metaphor most commonly associated with the Council was that of opening the windows of the Church to some fresh ideas. This was the response of John XXIII to an ambassador who asked what he was hoping to achieve. Coupled with the 'fresh air' metaphor was the slogan *'aggiornamento'* or renewal.

The problems of the pontificate of Paul VI (1963-1978) were not caused by fresh ideas or renewal *per se*. Rather the difficulty lay in examining such ideas and pastoral proposals within a theological framework. One historian has written that at the time of the Council 'we did not think to ask from it any consistent theoretical foundation for *aggiornamento*, because most of us were not aware of the importance of having one'.[1] As a consequence, 'the Council's fundamental injunction to remain faithful to the authentic past while adjusting to contemporary needs was transformed from a practical norm for reform into an explosive problematic.'[2] In a series of questions put to Paul VI by the Protestant theologian Karl Barth in 1966, Barth inquired, "What does *aggiornamento* mean? Accommodation to what?"[3]

In the absence of a clear theological framework for interpreting *aggiornamento*, Catholics throughout the world divided over the meaning of the Conciliar call to be 'relevant' to the needs of 'modern man'. Clergy and religious frequently interpreted the call as a mandate to throw off the symbols of their religious state, to don secular garb and blend in with the crowd. Catholic laity often interpreted the message to mean that they were no longer required to engage in political struggles with secularists but could privatise their faith and be catholic in denominational identity but liberal in cultural and political practice. These secularising tendencies were exacerbated in 1968 by the revolt of Catholic intellectuals against Paul VI's encyclical

[1] O' Malley, J, *Tradition and Transition: Historical Perspectives on Vatican II*, Wilmington, DE: M. Glazier, 1989, p. 45.
[2] *ibid*, p. 45
[3] Barth, K, *Ad Limina Apostolorum*, (Edinburgh: St. Andrew's Press, 1969), p. 20.

Humanae vitae which upheld the Church's teaching on contraception, and by the introduction of a new rite of the Mass which opened the liturgical arena to the same kind of confusion and secularising practices which were already rampant in other areas of ecclesial life. For many, a 'relevant' liturgy became a 'down-to-earth' casual celebration of the parish community as a good in itself.

As is typical of cultural revolutions, all symbols and idioms of the previous order were subject to suppression. High altars were destroyed and Catholic children in first world countries were no longer taught Latin hymns, but they were taught pigeon English songs such as the theologically facile "Kum-by-ya". The trend was to deem anything 'third world' or popular as 'relevant', while anything classical or requiring higher standards of learning was 'irrelevant' and 'pre-Conciliar'. In an era which coincided with the de-colonisation of Africa and the Pacific, many first world Catholics seemed to be embarrassed by their European cultural heritage and began succumbing to a cultural vision best described by Gabriel Motzkin, a Jewish scholar of modernity, as 'emotional primitivism'. Bernard Lonergan's criticisms of 'classicism' added fuel to this particular fire. At the same time members of missionary orders started to question the need for the evangelisation of non-Catholic peoples on the basis of Karl Rahner's theology of the 'anonymous Christian' and certain interpretations of the Conciliar documents on ecumenism and missionary work. It was popularly believed by some that the Council had endorsed the metaphor that God is like an elephant. Catholics have grasped his trunk, protestants his ears, Buddhists his tail and so on, but no one religious tradition had completely grasped the whole elephant.

In the midst of the turmoil many thousands of priests and religious abandoned their vocations while some small groups of laity in different ways tried to hold on to the pre-conciliar traditions. These groups were particularly strong in France where the words 'modern' and 'modernity' tend to be associated with the French Revolution, an event which was as anti-Catholic as anti-monarchist. For such people the idea that the Church might baptise a culture built over the bodies of some hundreds of thousands of martyrs could only come from Freemasonry or the devil himself. Some of these were ultimately to leave the Church in schism.

Such was the Church inherited by Cardinal Wojtyla in 1978. Its symbols were the American nun in shorts and T-shirt with a guitar slung over one shoulder and a book on Eastern meditation in the other hand; the 'just call me Kevin' sort of priest who was not sure what he believed about key doctrines but was certain that he had to be 'with it' wherever 'it' was; and groups of disgruntled laity who either wanted to return to the pre-Conciliar order or move towards a more liberal protestant ecclesial vision.

By personality John Paul II is a scholar with a strong sense of the dramatic. His first vocational orientation was towards acting. His personal style is not that of a general who rules by edicts, but a scholar-saint who leads by example and intellectual persuasion. Through a combination of appeals to reason, the authority of the magisterium, scripture and tradition, and his own personal witness, he has over the past 25 years established the broad contours of an intellectual framework for an authentic interpretation of the Council. It is an interpretation which places an emphasis on spiritual renewal and a continuation of the *Ressourcement* projects of Conciliar *periti* such as Cardinal Henri de Lubac. The *Ressourcement* circle of scholars believed that it was necessary to recover the wisdom of the patristics in order to deal with the intellectual challenges posed by the culture of modernity. Though not opposed to the Thomist tradition *per se*, they believed that the scholasticism dominant in seminaries of the pre-Conciliar era was on its own, an inadequate weapon for dealing with the intellectual complexities of modern atheism, and that in some instances it represented a seventeenth century distortion of the classical Thomist account of the relationship between nature and grace.

In his address to the Roman Curia on the thirtieth anniversary of the Council, John Paul II observed that a Council always takes place at a determined point in history, and therefore the historical context is important for understanding the meaning of Conciliar decrees. However, he added that a Council also springs up, as it were, 'from the subsoil of the Church's history, right from the beginning'.[4] This means that a Council can never represent a completely new start in the history of the Church, but rather a deepening and development of elements already present in its sacred history and tradition. Throughout the past quarter century a major aspect of his pontificate has therefore been the clarification, development and implementation of the decrees of the Council in a manner which perfects rather than destroys elements of pre-

[4] John Paul II, 'Address to the Roman Curia on Vatican Council II," *L'Osservatore Romano* (23 December 1992), p.6

Conciliar theology. This has been a central feature of his encyclicals and pastoral projects such as the Marian and Jubilee years and the promulgation of the *Catechism of the Catholic Church*.

In addition to John Paul II's encyclicals, exhortations and letters, which always refer back to Conciliar themes, another important contribution to the interpretation of the Council is the Report of the 1985 *Extraordinary Synod on the Celebration, Verification and Promotion of Vatican II* which he convened. In this document express reference is made to the concept of *aggiornamento* and to the fact that the term should never be construed as encouraging 'an easy accommodation that could lead to the secularisation of the Church'. Above all, in this document and many subsequent speeches, John Paul II has sought to counter the secularising interpretations of the Conciliar call for 'relevance' and 'renewal' by the development of a strong theological anthropology grounded in paragraph 22 of the Conciliar document *Gaudium et spes*.[5] The central principle of the paragraph is the following:

> The truth is that only in the mystery of the incarnate Word does the mystery of man take on light. For Adam, the first man, was a figure of Him who was to come, namely Christ the Lord. Christ, the final Adam, by the revelation of the mystery of the Father, and His Love, fully reveals man to man himself and makes his supreme calling clear. It is not surprising, then, that in Him all the aforementioned truths find their root and attain their crown.

[5] For an excellent overview of John Paul II's theological anthropology and its relationship to Vatican II, see, David Schindler, "Reorienting the Church on the Eve of the Millennium: John Paul II's 'New Evangelization'", *Communio* 24 (Winter, 1997): pp. 729-779.

This paragraph, which owes its origins to the pre-conciliar work *The Drama of Atheistic Humanism* by Henri de Lubac, a *peritus* (academic advisor) at the Council, friend of the then bishop Wojtyla, and co-author of sections of *Gaudium et spes*, places Christ at the very centre of human history and forms the basis for a theological anthropology and sociology. Not only has John Paul II constantly reiterated this passage of *Gaudium et spes* in his many homilies, but its theme was developed in his very first encyclical *Redemptor hominis*, which begins with the words, "Jesus Christ, the Redeemer of Man, is the centre and purpose of human history". Far from fostering an increasingly secularist vision of the purpose of the Church and human life, John Paul II has been a tireless campaigner against what he sees as the limitations of the various Enlightenment projects. In a typical address to the faculty of the Catholic University of Lublin (KUL), he stated that the reduction inherent in the Enlightenment view of man 'ushers in not only Nietzsche's issue of the death of God, but the prospect of the death of man who in such a materialistic vision of reality does not in the final, eschatological sense, have any possibilities other than those objects of the visible order'.[6]

A paradox to which many of the post-moderns have alluded is that whereas the various Enlightenments each in its own way began by marginalising God from social life and making the individual operating by an allegedly theologically neutral 'pure reason' the centre of the universe, contemporary scientific developments have turned against humanity with such intensity that there is

---

[6] John Paul II, "Speech to the Scholars of Lublin University," *Christian Life in Poland*, November 1987, p.52

now a need to protect the human person from the pretensions and projects of a rationality without God. John Paul II explains this by reference to the difficulty of individuals caught in a position where they are superior to other created things but still inferior to God:

> Man from the beginning is tempted to subordinate the truth about himself to the power of his own will by placing himself through that which is above good and evil; that is, he is tempted by the illusion that he will find the truth about good and evil only when he himself will decide about it. At the same time man is called from the beginning to bring the earth under his control which constitutes a natural fruit and at the same time practical extension of cognition or mastering of the rest of creatures.[7]

For John Paul II the tension between these two biblical commands is such that a reconciliation can only be achieved by adopting the position that in bringing the earth under control, one must respect the natural law - that rule of reason, promulgated by God in man's nature, whereby the human person can discern how he should act. Although the authors of the Conciliar documents played down the language of the natural law tradition so as not to offend the Protestant observers, throughout his various encyclicals, but particularly in *Veritatis splendor* (1993), John Paul II has made it clear that the natural law tradition is still very much a part of the Church's moral teaching.

---

[7] *ibid*, p. 51.

Accordingly, he argues that within each person there is a divine imprint, the contours of which provide the guidelines for discerning good from evil actions. The person who discerns these principles and acts according to them will reflect the goodness, truth and beauty of his or her divine pedigree. The human person however has the freedom to choose against the principles of the natural law, and may, as in the Genesis narrative, opt for the goods of the 'tree of knowledge of good and evil', over the goods of the 'tree of life'. More concretely, the choice is one between the overarching principles of power (as the fruit of the knowledge of good and evil) and love (the essence of the 'tree of life'), or, as David Schindler suggests, between Nietzsche's self-assertive *übermensch* (superman), or the *Theotokos* (Mother of God), with her receptivity to the will of God.

Whereas some sections of *Gaudium et spes* emphasised the achievements of 'modern man' to such a degree that Cardinal Ratzinger lamented that the terminology is 'downright Pelagian', and others complained that the document treated Christ more as *Omega* than as *Alpha*, John Paul II in various of his works has sought to clarify the ambiguity. In his apostolic letter *Tertio millennio adveniente* (10), he stressed that within Christianity time has a fundamental importance:

> Within the dimension of time the world was created; within it the history of salvation unfolds, finding its culmination in the 'fullness of time' of the Incarnation, and its goal in the glorious return of the Son of God at the end of time. In Jesus Christ, the Word made flesh, time becomes a dimension of God, who is Himself eternal...Christ, true God and true man, the Lord of the

cosmos, is also the Lord of history, of which he is 'the *Alpha* and the *Omega* (*Rev* 1:8, 21:6), the beginning and the end' (*Rev* 21:6)... From this relationship to God with time there arises the duty to sanctify time.

This notion of a duty to sanctify time and thereby acknowledge Christ as Lord and master of the temporal order runs counter to the immediate post-conciliar trend of severing the so-called natural and supernatural orders, privatising the supernatural, and making compromises with proponents of the liberal tradition to banish God from public discourse. In this context, John Paul II makes frequent reference to themes in the Conciliar document *Lumen gentium*, according to which the Church is the light of the nations and the universal sacrament of salvation. As such the Church has a mission in history and is not merely a provider of social and liturgical services for its members. Indeed, in a recent statement of the International Theological Commission, the theological anthropology of *Gaudium et spes* (22) is brought together with the ecclesiology of *Lumen gentium*:

> In the 'last times' inaugurated at Pentecost, the risen Christ, *Alpha* and *Omega*, enters into the history of peoples: from that moment, the sense of history and thus of culture is unsealed and the Holy Spirit reveals it by actualizing and communicating it to all. The Church is the sacrament of this revelation and its communication. It re-centers every culture into which Christ is received, placing it in the axis of the world which is coming and restores the union broken by the prince of this world. Culture is thus eschatologically

situated; it tends toward its completion in Christ, but it cannot be saved except by associating itself with the repudiation of evil.[8]

John Paul II is well aware that such a repudiation of evil involves suffering. He constantly reminds his audiences that the world is at a crossroad where it can either choose the principles of a civilisation of love, or alternatively, a culture of death. Implicit within this judgement is an understanding that cultures are built upon practices and that practices can either foster the good, the true and the beautiful, or be impediments to the same. In *Dominum et vivificantem* (56) he reminded the faithful that the resistance to the Holy Spirit within the human heart finds 'in every period in history and especially in the modern era its *external dimension*, which takes concrete form as the content of culture and civilisation, as *a philosophical* system, an ideology; *a programme* for action and for the shaping of human behaviour'. Accordingly, a Church which is relevant to the needs of contemporary man cannot be one which simply mimics the norms and practices of the surrounding culture. Any engagement with the realms of culture must be critical, and in particular, the practices upon which a culture is built must be open to the work of grace. The work of opposing the practices of the culture of death requires moral heroism, indeed sanctity, and even the possibility of martyrdom.

In *Evangelium vitae* (20) and (21) John Paul II diagnosed the root of the culture of death as a perverted notion of the

---

[8] International Theological Commission, "Faith and Inculturation", *Origins 18*, 47, 1989, p. 800-7.

meaning of human freedom. Freedom is construed as the emancipation of the will from all forms of tradition and authority. This excludes the truths of revelation. For John Paul II such a morally autonomous self is a tragic illusion based on a false anthropology. Moreover, he argues that this anthropology is 'typical of a social and cultural climate dominated by secularism, which, with its ubiquitous tentacles, succeeds at times in putting Christian communities themselves to the test.' While the language of *Gaudium et spes* was quite positive about the achievements of so-called 'modern man', John Paul II reminds his audiences that those sections of *Gaudium et spes* need to be read in conjunction with other passages in the document that acknowledge the situation of sin in the contemporary world and seek to explain its cause.[9]

Related to this false understanding of human freedom, has been an equally false and confused understanding of the rôle of the conscience in moral judgement. The Second Vatican Council mentioned the Catholic teaching on conscience when it spoke about man's vocation and in particular about the dignity of the human person. *Gaudium et spes* (16) also stated that 'in the depth of his conscience, man detects a law which he does not impose on himself, but which holds him to obedience'. There should not have been any ambiguity here. However, following the promulgation of *Humanae vitae*, it was popularly believed to be morally acceptable for Catholics to reject the teaching of this encyclical if in conscience they felt it right to do so. Thus, in *Veritatis splendor*, where John Paul II affirms the

---

[9] *Dominum et vivificantem* (29)

teaching of *Humanae vitae*, he asserts that the conscience is not an independent and exclusive capacity to decide what is good and evil, and he reiterates the observation of John Henry Newman, that the conscience only has rights because it has duties.

The reason that the conscience cannot be a law unto itself is again a matter of anthropology. As John Paul II states in *Veritatis splendor* (72), the morality of human acts is defined by the relationship of man's freedom with the authentic good. Acts which are not directed toward authentic goods cannot be made good by any so-called 'good motivation' or intention. Human freedom cannot create its own moral norms on the basis of historical contingencies or the diversity of societies and cultures, because the human person has been made in the image and likeness of God, that is, according to a divine pattern. Some things are good for man, or worthy ends for his actions and talents, while others are beneath his dignity, or, in the specific case of contraception, a rejection and mis-use of a gift.

John Paul II has however appreciated the intellectual and pastoral complexities of these issues. Although he agreed with the conclusions of Paul VI he did not think that the issue of contraception and of sexuality more generally had been adequately integrated into the larger question of the nature and destiny of the human being. For many readers of *Humanae vitae*, natural law was taken to mean merely the biological regularity found within the female reproductive system. His own work *Love and Responsibility* first published in 1961 approached these issues from a richer anthropological framework, but he still believed that an enormous amount of work needed to be done to deepen the faithful's understanding of these difficult questions. To this end in 1981 he established the first John Paul II Institute for Marriage and Family studies at the Lateran University in Rome. Its brief includes the development of a theological and philosophical anthropology in the light of the main doctrines of the Church, especially those in the fields of Christology, Trinitarian theology, Mariology and ecclesiology. Since 1981 other branches of the Institute have been established throughout the world with the three Anglophone Institutes being located in Washington D.C., Melbourne, Australia and Changanacherry, India.

A major feature of the work of these Institutes is the study of contemporary pastoral problems in the light of a spectrum of disciplines, including, and above all, theology. Whereas sections of *Gaudium et spes* were popularly interpreted as sanctioning scholarship without reference to theological and philosophical first principles, John Paul II constantly asserts that Catholic scholarship worthy of the name will never reach conclusions that are contrary to, or incompatible with, the truths of Revelation, especially the revelation about the divine pedigree of the human person. Thus, in *Fides et ratio* (61) he noted that on a number of occasions the Second Vatican Council stressed the positive value of scientific research for a deeper knowledge of the mystery of the human being, but he added that 'the invitation addressed to theologians to engage the human sciences and apply them properly in their inquiries should not be interpreted as an implicit authorisation to marginalise philosophy or to put something else in its place in pastoral formation and in the *praeparatio fidei*.'

In addition to drawing attention to the importance of the theological anthropology of *Gaudium et spes*, especially as it is expressed in paragraph 22, the Report of the 1985 Extraordinary Synod also states that the ecclesiology of communion, often called by its Latin name, *Communio*, is the central and fundamental idea of the Council's documents. This ecclesiology offers a vision of the Church as a series of interconnected and mutually supporting relationships, analogous to the relations and community within the Trinity. A year later in *Dominum et vivificantem* (29) John Paul II reiterated this judgement when he observed that the Second Vatican Council was in an especial way an ecclesiological council - a council on the theme of the Church.

The term *Communio* is associated both with the Council's ecclesiology, which, like the theological anthropology of *Gaudium et spes* (22), owes much to the pre-Conciliar work of Henri de Lubac, and also with a journal published in some 15 different language editions throughout the world. The journal's founders included the great Swiss theologian Hans Urs von Balthasar, de Lubac, Joseph Ratzinger, and the Pope himself. It has since developed into *the* most significant journal of contemporary Catholic theology in line with the teachings of the magisterium. Scholars who currently write for the journal tend to build on the work of the *Ressourcement* circle and on von Balthasar's notion of a symphony of spiritual traditions and missions in the life of the Church, especially the Petrine, Marian and Johannine missions, which have done much to enrich and expand the notion of *Communio*. Speaking of the *Communio* project, David

Schindler has said that the retrieval of Catholic sources to deal with contemporary theological and pastoral challenges in the life of the Church 'requires a kind of reversal, turning our post-Enlightenment thought patterns upside down and inserting ourselves inside revelation - and through prayer, obedience and participation in the life of the Church, reading culture from a Christological point of view.' In other words, it involves 'reading the signs of the times through the mind of God'. This is also the position of Cardinal Stafford, the President of the Pontifical Council for the Laity, who is also associated with the *Communio* project. In a recent interview he stated that 'the crisis in the Church will continue until the Catholic Church comes to a deeper awareness and consciousness - and above all judgement - about the compatibility of elements within modern culture and the Catholic faith' and that a fundamental question is whether modern culture is a *praeparatio evangelica* (preparation for the gospel) or not?[10] The project is thus one of working within the broad contours of John Paul II's interpretation of the Council to develop the Church's intellectual resources for understanding such problems as modernity, post-modernity, the culture of death and the meaning of masculinity and femininity.

Ambiguities about the nature of the Church flowing from some of the terminological looseness of the Conciliar documents have also been addressed in the document *Dominus Iesus*, a declaration of the Congregation for the Doctrine of the Faith, ratified and confirmed by John Paul II.

---

[10] Cardinal Stafford, Interview with Antonio Enrique of *The Pilot*, Archdiocese of Boston, August 8, 2003.

This declaration begins with the observation that the Church's constant missionary proclamation is endangered by relativistic theories which seek to justify religious pluralism, not only *de facto* but also *de iure* (or in principle). In other words, theories such as 'God is like an elephant' with different religious denominations and traditions having grasped different parts of the elephant, are an example of positions which are in principle, not just in consequence, relativist. Contrary to such positions, the document declares that the Catholic faithful are *required to profess* that there is an historical continuity - rooted in the apostolic succession - between the Church founded by Christ and the Catholic Church:

> This is the single Church of Christ ... which our Saviour, after his resurrection, entrusted to Peter's pastoral care (*cf: Jn* 21:17), commissioning him and the other Apostles to extend and rule her (*cf: Mt* 28:18*ff*), erected for all ages as 'the pillar and mainstay of the truth' (*1 Tim* 3:15). This Church, constituted and organised as a society in the present world, subsists in the Catholic Church, governed by the successor of Peter and by the Bishops in communion with him.[11]

The words 'subsists in' come from the Conciliar document *Lumen gentium*. In *Dominus Iesus* it is stated that with this expression the Second Vatican Council sought to harmonize two doctrinal statements: on the one hand, that the Church of Christ, despite the divisions which exist

---

[11] Congregation for the Doctrine of the Faith, Declaration on the Unicity and Salvific Universality of Jesus Christ and the Church, *Dominus Iesus* (16), (Catholic Truth Society: London, 2000) , p. 21.

among Christians, continues to exist fully only in the Catholic Church, and on the other hand, that outside of her structure, many elements can be found of sanctification and truth, that is, in those Churches and ecclesial communities which are not yet in full communion with the Catholic Church.[12] In case there be any lingering ambiguity, footnote 56 of the document declares:

> the interpretation of those who would derive from the formula *subsistit in* the thesis that the one Church of Christ could subsist also in non-Catholic churches is contrary to the authentic meaning of *Lumen gentium*.

Moreover, according to *Dominus Iesus*, the Catholic faithful are not permitted to imagine that the Church of Christ is nothing more than a collection of Churches and ecclesial communities, (as members of a congregationalist community might believe), nor are they free to hold that the Church of Christ nowhere really exists, and must be considered only as a goal which all ecclesial communities must strive to reach.[13] On the contrary, Catholics must hold as contrary to the faith, theological propositions which deny the unicity of the relationship between Christ and the Church and the kingdom of God.[14] Accordingly, the inter-religious dialogue which has been fostered by the Conciliar decree on Ecumenism is just one of the actions of the Church in her mission to the unconverted. It is not an exercise in working out what bits of other religious traditions are insights hitherto unavailable to Catholics which should be incorporated into the Catholic tradition.

[12] *Dominus Iesus* (16)
[13] *Dominus Iesus* (17)
[14] *Dominus Iesus* (19).

Catholics have access to the whole elephant, not just the trunk, ears or tail.

Implicit within *Dominus Iesus* is a rejection of a sociological reading of the Church by which it is viewed rather like a large multinational corporation with the Pope as its chief executive officer, the hierarchy the executive staff and the laity the shareholders. In his most recent encyclical, *Ecclesia de eucharistia*, John Paul II has also rejected a sociological or functionalist reading of the priesthood. Referring to the Council's use of the distinction between the laity as members of the royal priesthood and the ordained priest who 'acting in the person of Christ, brings about the Eucharistic Sacrifice and offers it to God in the name of all the people', he asserts that 'the Eucharistic mystery cannot be celebrated in any community except by an ordained priest, as the Fourth Lateran Council expressly taught'.[15] Accordingly, the idea of a 'priestless parish' run by lay pastoral associates is not part of John Paul II's ecclesial vision for the era of new evangelisation. Moreover, he argues that the phrase *in persona Christi* means more than offering in the name of, or in the place of, Christ. *In persona* means 'in specific sacramental identification with the eternal High Priest who is the author and principal subject of this sacrifice of his, a sacrifice in which, in truth, nobody can take his place'. The Eucharist which the ordained priests celebrate is a '*gift which radically transcends the power of the assembly* and is in any event essential for validly linking the Eucharistic consecration to the sacrifice of the Cross and to the Last Supper.'[16]

[15] *Ecclesia de eucharistia* (29).
[16] *Ibid*, (29).

Although John Paul II has not developed what might be called a 'theology of culture', which is arguably a necessary scholarly project for the Church at this time in her history when she needs to critically assess elements of modern and post-modern culture; he has certainly affirmed the continuing relevance of elements of pre-Conciliar Catholic culture. In *Fides et ratio* (72) he argued that in 'engaging great cultures for the first time the Church cannot abandon what she has gained from her inculturation in the world of Greco-Latin thought', for 'to reject this heritage would be to deny the providential plan of God who guides His Church down the paths of time and history.' Even more recently at a 2002 conference called to mark the fortieth anniversary of the promulgation of *Veterum sapientia*, the 1962 document of John XXIII which endorsed the use of Latin, 'not merely as a passport to a proper understanding of the Christian writers of antiquity, or from a desire for bureaucratic uniformity, but as an element of the Church's tradition which is valuable for 'religious reasons',' John Paul II referred to a knowledge of Latin as the 'indispensable condition for a proper relationship between modernity and antiquity, for dialogue among cultures, and for reaffirming the identity of the Catholic priesthood.'[17] Both of these statements run counter to the intellectual fashions of the 1960's and 1970's to regard anything classical or culturally universal as 'irrelevant'.

Speaking of the period between the Council and the year 2000, John Paul II suggests that what has been accomplished is the preparation for a new springtime of

---

[17] Catholic World News Report, *AD 2000*. (15, 3, 2002), p. 5

Christian life. This, he acknowledges, will be the inheritance of the younger generation of today's Catholics.[18] Their greatest obstacles, apart from the culture of death itself and its life denying practices, are the attitudes of their generation of '1968' superiors who still wield enormous influence within the pastoral and educational institutions of the Church. For many members of this older generation, Vatican II remains in their memory as a kind of ecclesiastical Woodstock. In this situation what is required is the work of scholar-saints who can make the forms of a Catholic culture visible in a splendor at once ancient and new. Among these, John Paul II will no doubt come to rank as one of the greatest. For his contribution to the interpretation of the Council, in particular for his development of de Lubac's ecclesiology and theological anthropology, and his application of the anthropology to the difficult topics in sexual ethics, and his defence of the priesthood and the Church against all sociological deconstructions which would reduce them to a collection of functions and social services; John Paul II may also one day rank as a Doctor of the Church.

After 25 years the symbols of this papacy are: Mother Teresa's sisters nursing the poor and dying; young religious of the old ecclesial Orders reading the patristics in all their narrative beauty, appreciating the logical rigour of the scholastics, being fully conversant with the great theological themes of von Balthasar, de Lubac, and other leaders of the *Ressourcement* and *Communio* circles, and defending the Church's teachings in the various *areopagi* of

---

[18] *Tertio millennio adveniente* (18)

the world in their radically pre-modern habits; and young laity of both new and old ecclesial movements working in the world to build flourishing families, protect the aged and unborn, sanctify time, and restore all things to Christ. To them his message is simply, "Be not afraid, the gates of hell cannot prevail". Through the Cross to Glory!

III

THE RADICALISM OF THE PAPACY:
JOHN PAUL II AND THE NEW
ECCLESIAL MOVEMENTS

Ian Ker

It is often said that G. K. Chesterton, who did not even have a university degree, was the author of the best studies ever to be written of such disparate figures as Thomas Aquinas and Dickens. This self-taught genius was neither a church historian nor a theologian, and yet in his book on *Chaucer* (1932) he wrote this remarkable passage on the radicalism of the papacy:

> It will be found again and again, in ecclesiastical history, that the new departure, the daring innovation, the progressive party, depended directly on the Pope. It was naturally more or less negatively resisted by the bishops, the canons, the clergy in possession ... Official oligarchies of that sort generally do resist reform and experiment ... But whenever there appeared, in Catholic history, a new and promising experiment, bolder or broader or more enlightened than existing routine, that movement always came to be identified with the Papacy; because the Papacy alone upheld it ... So ... it was really

the Pope who upheld St. Francis and the popular movement of the Friars. So, in the sixteenth century, it was really the Pope who upheld St. Ignatius Loyola and the great educational movement of the Jesuits. The Pope, being the ultimate court of appeal, cannot for shame be a mere expression of any local prejudice; this may easily be strong among local ecclesiastics, without any evil intention; but the remote arbiter at Rome must make some attempt to keep himself clear of it.[1]

Cardinal Joseph Ratzinger made exactly the same point in his address to the 1998 World Congress of the Ecclesial Movements in Rome. Reflecting on 'the successive waves of movements that renew the universalistic aspect of her apostolic mission and thus serve to foster the spiritual vitality and truth of the local Churches', he pointed out that, 'The papacy did not create the movements, but it did become their most important backer in the structure of the Church, their main source of ecclesial support.' From this fact of history, he drew an important ecclesiological conclusion: 'Perhaps the deepest meaning and true nature of the petrine office as a whole was in this way brought into view: namely, that the Bishop of Rome is not merely the bishop of a local Church; his ministry is always referred to the universal Church. It has thus, in a specific sense, an apostolic character. It must keep alive the dynamism of the Church's mission ...' Not surprisingly, then, 'Movements that transcended the scope and structure of the local Church ... went increasingly in hand with the papacy.'

[1] *The Collected Works of G. K. Chesterton*, vol. XVIII (San Francisco: Ignatius Press, 1991), 186.

Thus from Gregory the Great to Gregory III, the papacy encouraged and supported monasticism, the first great movement that begins in the third century. Just as these popes saw the missionary potential of monasticism, so too the mendicant movements of Francis of Assisi and Dominic in the thirteenth century 'found their support in the holder of an universal ecclesial ministry, in the Pope as guarantee of the mission and the upbuilding of the one Church'. And this had the important ecclesiological effect of developing the doctrine of papal primacy, which 'was understood anew in the light of its apostolic roots'.

After touching on the apostolic movements of evangelisation that began in the sixteenth century, particularly that of the Society of Jesus, and the missionary congregations of the nineteenth century, Ratzinger again stressed that these movements which serve the universal mission of the Church and not merely the local Church are essential to the Church and the pope has 'to rely on them' and 'they on him'. These apostolic movements differ from each other 'because they are the Holy Spirit's answer to the ever changing situations in which the Church lives'. They 'generally derive their origin from a charismatic leader and take shape in concrete communities, inspired by the life of their founder; they attempt to live the Gospel anew, in its totality'.[2]

Ratzinger is in no doubt that in our own times the Church is again enjoying another great charismatic experience in the form of the new so-called 'ecclesial movements'. At the beginning of his address he quoted the

---

[2] Joseph Ratzinger, 'The Ecclesial Movements: A Theological reflection on their place in the Church', *Movements in the Church: Proceedings of the World Congress of the Ecclesial Movements, Rome, 27-29 May 1998* (Vatican City: Pontificium Consilium pro Laicis, 1999), 39-40, 43, 46-8.

reference in Pope John Paul II's encyclical *Redemptoris missio* (1990) to 'a new development ... the rapid growth of "ecclesial movements" filled with missionary dynamism', which 'represent a true gift from God both for new evangelisation and for missionary activity ... I therefore recommend that they be spread, and that they be used to give fresh energy, especially among young people, to the Christian life and to evangelisation ...' And Ratzinger enthusiastically echoed the Pope's words: 'For me personally it was a wonderful experience when, in the early 1980s, I first came into close contact with movements such as the *Neocatechumenal Way, Communion and Liberation* and the *Focolare Movement*, and so experienced the energy and enthusiasm with which they lived their faith and the joy of their faith ... That was the period in which Karl Rahner and others were speaking of a winter in the Church; and, indeed, it did seem that, after the great flowering of the Council, spring had been reclaimed by frost, and that the new dynamism had succumbed to exhaustion.'

But Ratzinger concluded his address by recognising that yet again it was the papacy above all which deserved credit for the 'discernment of spirits' in the matter of the new movements: 'Above all ... let us thank Pope John Paul II. He surpasses us all in his capacity for enthusiasm ...' Nor does it require much reading between the lines to sense the contrast Ratzinger makes between this papal encouragement and support and the suspicion or even hostility of many local bishops. While warning the movements against any kind of élitism or exclusivism, the Cardinal's warning to local churches and bishops is noticeably more lengthy and pointed, for he sees history repeating itself:

> ... the local Churches ... even the bishops, must be reminded that they must avoid any uniformity of pastoral organisations and programmes. They must not turn their own pastoral plans into the criterion of what the Holy Spirit is allowed to do: an obsession with planning could render the Churches impervious to the action of the Holy Spirit ... Not everything should be fitted into the straight jacket of a single uniform organisation; what is needed is less organisation and more Spirit! Above all, a concept of *communio*, in which the highest pastoral value is attached to the avoidance of conflict, should be rejected. Faith remains a sword and may demand conflict for the sake of truth and love.[3]

Pope John Paul II, then, is continuing a long papal tradition of encouraging and fostering charismatic initiatives that all too often have met with opposition from local bishops and clergy. This is obviously partly due to conservatism, inertia, and the preference for the status quo. There is also the very human desire by local church leaders to exercise a control that goes beyond their perfectly legitimate duty and responsibility as pastors to discern the genuineness of charisms.

But there is also a very important theological issue at stake. And again John Paul II has understood much better than many bishops the radicalism of the ecclesiology of the Second Vatican Council. In his address to the 1998 congress

---

[3] Ratzinger, *op. cit.*, 23-4, 50-51.

the Pope pointed out that the Council 'rediscovered the charismatic dimension as one of [the Church's] constitutive elements'. The constitution on the Church, *Lumen gentium*, speaks specifically of the charismatic dimension of the Church three times in the first two chapters. In chapter 1 it says that the Holy Spirit bestows upon the Church 'varied hierarchic and charismatic gifts' (4), adding later that among the 'gifts' given by the Spirit 'the primacy belongs to the grace of the apostles to whose authority the Spirit himself subjects even those who are endowed with charisms' (7). The second chapter contains a longer passage from which the Pope quoted in his address:

> It is not only through the sacraments and ministrations of the Church that the Holy Spirit makes holy the people, leads them and enriches them with his virtues. Allotting his gifts according as he wills (*cf. 1 Cor* 12:11), he also distributes special graces among the faithful of every rank. By these gifts he makes them fit and ready to undertake various tasks and offices for the renewal and building up of the Church, as it is written, 'the manifestation of the Spirit is given to everyone for profit' (*1 Cor* 12:7). Whether these charisms be very remarkable or more simple and widely diffused, they are to be received with thanksgiving and consolation since they are fitting and useful for the needs of the Church. (12)

Having emphasised this rediscovery of the charismatic dimension, the Pope is careful to add that, 'The institutional and charismatic aspects are co-essential as it were to the Church's constitution. They contribute, although differently, to the life, renewal and sanctification of God's People.' But, in view of the rise of ecclesial movements and new communities before and after the Council, the Pope can say that 'this ... rediscovery of the Church's charismatic dimension' has proved to be 'providential'.[4]

This papal teaching on *Lumen gentium's* teaching on the charisms, which represented a victory for the reformers at the Council, is of great importance. It decisively corrects a misinterpretation of these crucial texts which was the accepted interpretation immediately after the Council thanks to an influential article in the liberal review *Concilium* by Hans Küng, which he subsequently incorporated in his well-known book *The Church* (1967). The article indeed appeared in 1965, the year the Council ended, and two years later in a standard commentary on the documents of Vatican II the distinguished theologian Aloys Grillmeier simply quoted Küng as the accepted authority on the Council's meaning.

> The *charismata* are not primarily extraordinary but common; they are not of one kind, but manifold; they are not limited to a special group of persons, but truly universal in the Church. All this implies also that they are not a thing of the past (possible and real only in the early Church), but eminently contemporary and actual; they do not hover on the periphery of the Church but are eminently central and essential to it. In this sense one should speak of a *charismatic structure of the Church* which embraces and goes beyond the structure of its government.[5]

[4] *Movements in the Church*, 221.
[5] *Commentary on the Documents of Vatican II*, vol. 2. ed. Herbert Vorgrimler (London: Burnes & Oates, 1967), 165.

However, in a more considered reassessment twenty-five years after the Council, the Biblical exegete Albert Vanhoye is sharply critical of what was taken in the immediate aftermath of the Council to be the authoritative explanation of what *Lumen gentium* meant by charisms. His article may be taken as a commentary on the Pope's words. He begins by pointing out that, while 'The concept of charisms has its starting point in certain New Testament texts that speak of *charisma*', nevertheless in Western theology 'the generalised use of the technical term "charism" is of relatively recent date', in view of the fact that the 'word is found only twice in the Vulgate', whereas elsewhere the word is translated by several different words. When Latin theologians following St Thomas Aquinas want to speak of charism they use the phrase '*gratia gratis data*'. With Vatican II, the vocabulary changes, since the official conciliar texts, written in Latin, use the Latin transliteration of the Greek word, except in quotations from the New Testament where the Vulgate is used. At the Council itself, there was a debate between the traditionalist view that charisms are extraordinary, miraculous gifts and that of the reformers who successfully pressed for charisms to be seen as much more ordinary gifts belonging to baptised Christians, such as the gifts of catachesis and evangelisation. It was this position that prevailed in *Lumen gentium* and to which John Paul remains faithful.

This is quite different from Küng's interpretation of charisms which Vanhoye regards as unfaithful to the conciliar texts and over-dependent on an influential study of '*Ministry and Community*' (1964) by the Protestant theologian E. Kasemann. Thus, Küng uncritically accepts the concept of charism as describing all ecclesial services and functions. Vanhoye points out that Küng so broadens the notion of charism as to rob it of any 'identifying characteristic'.

For example, Küng sees Christian love as the highest as well as the most ordinary of the charisms. But Vanhoye argues that this is only possible if we take charism to mean simply a gift as opposed to 'a special grace granted to one Christian and not to another'. But it is manifest that when Vatican II rediscovered the charismatic dimension, to use the Pope's words, it was doing something more significant than saying that all the Christian virtues are gifts. If that was all that *Lumen gentium* intended in those three texts in the first two chapters, then the dispute between the reformers led by Cardinal Suenens and the conservatives led by Cardinal Ruffini was pointless, as both sides would have agreed that the Christian virtues are gifts. But the issue was whether or not ordinary Christians can possess special charisms which help to build up the Church, or whether the Church is to be seen as sustained primarily and for the most part (except in extraordinary and miraculous instances) by the ministry and sacraments of the ordained priesthood. But, as Vanhoye sarcastically puts it, 'meekly' following the Protestant Kasemann, Küng sees charisms everywhere, and so evacuates the term of any special meaning that 'it loses any substance and it becomes difficult to see how the charisms could then provide the Church with a "structure"'.

Now Küng, of course, has a very definite agenda in extending the sense of charism, and that is, to quote Vanhoye again, his anxiety 'to limit the sphere of responsibility of the pastors of the Church as much as possible'. Insistent that charisms are not the preserve of the hierarchy, 'he describes everything as a charism, from theological charity to the actions of eating and drinking. In this way, the authorities of the Church are, so to speak, drowned in an ocean of charisms possessed by all the members of the faithful.' But then, Küng introduces another concept of charisms, as the personal gifts belonging to individuals called to a particular ministry within the Church. This is the basis for his idea of a 'charismatic structure' of the Church, which is very different from saying that the Church has a charismatic dimension. But the Church also has a hierarchical dimension, indeed structure, which, according to *Lumen gentium*, discerns and regulates the charismatic dimension: 'Those who have charge over the Church should judge the genuineness and proper use of these gifts, through their office not indeed to extinguish the Spirit, but to test all things and hold fast to what is good.' (12)

This specific teaching of the Council is ignored by Küng, unsurprisingly. To the question as to how unity is to be preserved in the kind of charismatic Church that Küng envisages, he replies that the same Spirit who gives the charisms also creates unity and order. This is certainly true, but the Spirit acts through the hierarchical dimension, as Paul says in 1 Corinthians: 'In the Church, God has given the first place to apostles, the second to prophets, the third to teachers; after them miracles, and after them the gift of healing; helpers, good leaders, those with many languages.' (12: 28)

These are precisely the 'varied hierarchic and charismatic gifts' of *Lumen gentium*, where hierarchy also takes precedence over charism. Paul himself gives concrete examples of ways in which apostolic authority is to be exercised with regard to the charisms, and adds that what he writes 'is a command from the Lord'. (14: 27-9, 37) As an exegete himself, Vanhoye concludes that, while in the New Testament the Greek word *charisma* often has only too general or too specific meaning of gift to be translated by the word charism, nevertheless there are clear instances of *charisma* being used to describe a special gift given to an individual for the good of the Church, and it is this usage which the Council employs, 'following a theological tradition'.[6]

It is paradoxical that, while Küng certainly intends the hierarchical dimension of the Church to be undermined by the charismatic dimension, in actual fact, by evacuating the charisms of all real significance, not only is the concept thoroughly devalued, but the result is effectively to restore that very clerical understanding of the Church which *Lumen gentium* intended to modify by the introduction of the charismatic dimension. For if everything is charismatic, then nothing is charismatic, and effectively we are back in a Church where in practice 'only ... the sacraments and the ministrations' count for anything. The consequence is that those who do not possess the sacrament of Holy Orders are in practice seen as second-class citizens, since 'the sacraments and ministrations' are the responsibility of the clergy. This is why, for instance, the progressivist

---

[6] Albert Vanhoye SJ, 'The Biblical Question of "Charisms" after Vatican II', in *Vatican II: Assessment and Perspectives: Twenty-five Years After (1962-1987)*, vol. 1, ed. Rene Latourelle (Mahwah, NJ: Paulist Press, 1988), 439-468.

position holds that it is essential that married men and women should be ordained to the priesthood. The devaluation of the charismatic dimension leads in effect to the old pre-Vatican II clerical model of the Church.

Pope John Paul II, on the contrary, fully appreciates the significance of *Lumen gentium's* texts on the charisms, without naturally in any way devaluating the hierarchical dimension. He regards, as we have seen, the two aspects as 'co-essential' and complementary. Charisms need hierarchy if they are not to run wild, and hierarchy needs charisms if it is not to fossilize. John Paul has a thoroughly Vatican II concept of the organic model of the Church that we find in the first two chapters of *Lumen gentium*, where the Council, which was very largely a council about the Church, sets out its fundamental understanding of the essential nature of the Church. This is not a Church which consists foremost and simply of clergy and laity, let alone clergy set against laity. Instead, these first two chapters are revolutionary, in the sense of rolling back, in the literal Latin sense of the word, the Church to its original identity as defined in Scripture and the Fathers.

In his apostolic exhortation *Christifideles laici* (1989), the Pope emphasises *Lumen gentium's* ecclesiology of communion, which it summarises in its opening paragraph: 'The Church in Christ is a kind of sacrament, that is, a sign and instrument of intimate union with God and of the unity of all the human race.' (1) This ecclesial communion is an 'organic' communion, which 'is characterised by a *diversity* and a *complementarity* of vocations and states in life, of ministries, of charisms and responsibilities' (20). And the Pope goes on to quote from *Lumen gentium* the second passage which refers to 'those who are endowed with charisms' but who are subjected by the Spirit to the apostles in the body of Christ with its 'diversity of members and functions' (7). It is the Spirit who ensures, the Pope stresses, '*the dynamic principle of diversity and unity* in the Church' (20), that same Spirit which 'bestows upon her varied hierarchical and charismatic gifts' (4).

The Pope, as we have seen, refers to the new movements as *ecclesial* not *lay* movements, and this reflects his understanding of their organic nature. Of course, the majority of the members of the movements are indeed lay, but they also include bishops, clergy, religious, as well as those lay members who assume such a degree of commitment to the particular charism of the movement as involves embracing chastity, obedience, and poverty, even if this commitment is not canonical. That organic community of the baptised with their different and varied ministries and charisms which is described in the first two chapters of *Lumen gentium* is realised in a particularly concrete and manifest way in the movements. As the Pope remarks in *Christifideles laici*, the Spirit gives charisms 'as a response to the varied needs of the Church in history' (24).

The founders of the movements, some of which pre-date Vatican II, were naturally not consciously responding to the teaching of *Lumen gentium*, which is a hierarchical document, but they were responding to the Spirit in putting, as it were, flesh and blood on the conciliar text. For the fact is that before - and indeed sadly since - the Council, the normal Catholic practice has been division rather than unity, with clergy on the one side and laity on the other. Religious were also a separate category, although the male orders and congregations had been largely clericalised, even where the original charism had not necessarily implied ministerial priesthood. After all, neither St Benedict nor St Francis were ordained to the priesthood. Still, leaving aside religious, the Church was - and still is - seen to consist primarily of clergy and laity. But 'lay' is a negative term describing someone who is not a cleric, with the implication that the lay person is an amateur Christian compared to the ordained priest. Priesthood is then seen as the fulfilment of baptism, not only by pre-Vatican II traditionalists but also, as I have pointed out, by progressive Catholics, to whom the exclusion of any class of persons from ministerial priesthood is manifestly unjust. But this was not St Paul's definition of the body of Christ, for whom the Church consisted of the baptised, among whom the apostles had first place, but not because the other members were just laity but because the apostles had the responsibility for discerning and authenticating the various charisms and ministries of their fellow Christians. This is the Church of *Lumen gentium* - at least in the first two chapters - and it is also the Church of John Paul, as it is of the movements.

The fact that the ecclesial movements are regularly referred to as *lay* movements indicates the old thinking about the Church as divided into clergy and laity. But, as Piero Coda, a theologian belonging to the *Focolare* movement, explains, 'ecclesiality' is 'a constituent feature of the movements'. To describe them as lay movements is not only factually inaccurate but also ecclesiologically false: for 'The new movements are constitutionally open (by virtue of their original charism) to all the vocations and to all the states of life present in the People of God.' And so the description of them as 'lay' movements is wholly 'reductive', since they not only in fact but in theory embrace all the baptised. To insist, therefore, on their correct description is not mere academic pedantry, as many might think on the ground that, after all, they do (inevitably) include far more laity than clergy and religious. Indeed, Coda calls their common classification as lay movements, 'inertia of reflection'. But I think we can be more precise than that: the misdescription reflects that separation of clergy from laity, from which the first two chapters of *Lumen gentium* sought to free the Church. The movements are ecclesial or movements of the Church in manifesting the same ecclesiology of organic wholeness.

The point is too important not to risk the danger of labouring it. For it is not just that the movements do in fact include priests and religious within them - although this certainly shows, in Coda's words, that 'the charism that lies at the origin of the movements is not in conflict, for example, with the spirituality and ministerial obligations of the priesthood nor with the charism of the consecrated life aroused and shaped according to the various spiritualities'. But, more fundamentally, the movements represent the concrete realisation - undecreed, unplanned by councils or synods or committees - of that idea of communion that lies at the heart of Vatican II's understanding of the Church. What we see in them, in Coda's words again, is the actuality of communion among the baptised, whereby 'the equal baptismal dignity and the complementarity of the various vocations, ministries and charisms' are made authentically possible 'in an organically and hierarchically structured communion'.[7]

[7] *Movements in the Church*, 95-6.

Pope John Paul II has fully understood both the communion theology of *Lumen gentium* and its realisation in the ecclesial movements. And it is no coincidence that so-called liberal Catholics who denounce him for undermining the Council are the same people who regard the rise of the movements with astonished horror. Surely, we are told, this outburst of evangelisation from the grassroots, radically innovative but also strongly orthodox and loyal to the Pope, is not in 'the spirit of Vatican II'. Now it is certainly true that evangelisation was not a theme of Vatican II; but, as I have written elsewhere, in the thought of John Henry Newman who is often called 'the Father of Vatican II', there are two kinds of development, very different from each other, which may follow a council. On the one hand, theological ideas become clearer and purer in the course of time, which would suggest that the profound communion theology of those first two chapters of *Lumen gentium* would not be so self-evident in the aftermath of the Council as the two more obvious chapters on episcopal collegiality and the laity.

On the other hand, however, there is another kind of post-conciliar development altogether; for it is not only a question of the meaning and significance of the fundamental ecclesiology of *Lumen gentium* becoming more luminous in retrospect and time, but there is also the consideration that councils open up further developments because, as Newman points out, of what they do *not* say. That is to say, one council will have a particular agenda at a particular point in time, but the next council will have another agenda, if only because the previous council may need modifying by the statement of complementary and supplementary truths. Thus Vatican II modified Vatican I's definition of papal infallibility with a much larger teaching about the whole Church, and especially the episcopate. In the event, it was not another council but a different pope from the pope who called the Council, who, nine years after the completion of Vatican II, turned the Church in a new direction with his call for a new evangelisation in *Evangelii nuntiandi* (1974). Now the new ecclesial movements can be seen as the concrete embodiment of *both* these two kinds of development: on the one hand, they exemplify in a particularly concrete and evident way the communion ecclesiology of *Lumen gentium*, while on the other hand they represent a powerful response to the call for a new evangelisation.[8]

Pope John Paul is in no doubt about the 'missionary dynamism' of the movements. Already in 1990 he noted their 'rapid growth' in his encyclical *Redemptoris missio*: '... they represent a true gift of God both for a new evangelisation and for missionary activity ... I therefore recommend that they be spread, and that they be used to give fresh energy, especially among people, to the Christian life and to evangelisation ...' (72). At the 1998 congress, he pointed out the 'urgent need for powerful proclamation and solid, in-depth Christian formation' to counteract the secularised culture'. And he went on to speak of another aspect of the movements, for mere preaching and education are not enough in a dechristianised society: there was a 'great need for living Christian communities'. And the Pope's joy is palpable as he exclaimed:

---

[8] See Ian Ker, 'Newman, Councils, and Vatican II', in Ian Ker and Terrence Merrigan, ed., *Newman and Faith* (Louvain: Peeters Press; Sterling, Virginia: W. B. Eerdmans, forthcoming 2004).

'And here are the movements and the new ecclesial communities: they are the response, given by the Holy Spirit, to this critical challenge at the end of the millennium.'

Two years earlier, again on the eve of Pentecost, he had said in a homily: 'One of the gifts of the Spirit to our time is undoubtedly the flourishing of the ecclesial movements which right from the beginning of my pontificate I have continued to indicate as a source of hope for the Church and for man.' However, the 1998 congress, which was the first meeting of all the movements with the Pope, was, he affirmed, a 'truly unprecedented event'. In his message to the congress, he called the movements 'one of the most significant fruits of that springtime in the Church which was foretold by the Second Vatican Council, but which unfortunately has often been hampered by the spread of secularisation'. And in his address at the end of the congress, he authenticated the charisms which have inspired the movements:

The ecclesial realities to which you belong have helped you to rediscover your baptismal vocation, to appreciate the gifts of the Spirit received at Confirmation, to entrust yourselves to God's forgiveness in the sacrament of Reconciliation and to recognise the Eucharist as the source and summit of all Christian life. Thanks to this powerful ecclesial experience, wonderful Christian families have come into being which are open to life, true "domestic churches", and many vocations to the ministerial priesthood and the religious life have blossomed, as well as new forms of lay life inspired by the evangelical counsels. You have learned in the movements and new communities that faith is not abstract talk, nor vague religious sentiment, but new life in Christ instilled by the Holy Spirit.[9]

The Pope is well aware that the local churches and pastors are frequently indifferent, not to say hostile, to the movements. This is the lesson of history, so clearly appreciated by Chesterton and Ratzinger. Of course, John Paul is also aware that new charisms carry their own problems. In his message to the 1998 congress, however, he detected 'a more mature self-knowledge'. And in his address at the end of the congress he affirmed a new 'ecclesial maturity', while acknowledging that the movements had 'given rise to questions, uneasiness and tensions; at times to presumptions and excesses'.

But on the other hand, the Pope also noted that there had been 'numerous prejudices' against them. It is clear that he expects bishops to follow his petrine primacy in the discernment of the new charisms: '... these charisms deserve attention from every member of the ecclesial community, beginning with the Pastors to whom the care of the particular Churches is entrusted in communion with the Vicar of Christ.' The implication of the Pope's words at the 1998 congress is that while the movements have gained in maturity, the local churches and bishops have not shown a corresponding growth in understanding, for, he pointedly remarks, the movements remain 'something new that is still waiting to be properly accepted and appreciated'.[10]

---

[9] *Movements in the Church*, 51, 9, 220, 16, 223.
[10] *Movements in the Church*, 16, 222, 18, 16.

And so Pope John Paul II, following, it has to be said, the early lead given by Pope Paul VI, is firmly in the tradition of the popes who, at critical times in the Church's life, have discerned dramatic new ways in which the Spirit has raised up new charismatic movements for the renewal and the propagation of the Christian faith.

IV

TOTUS TUUS:
THE MARIOLOGY OF
JOHN PAUL II

Brendan Leahy

Launching out into the deep, at the very beginning of his pontificate, John Paul II's choice of the simple motto, *Totus Tuus* ('I am completely yours, Mary') showed he was intent on being a 'Marian Pope'. Twenty-five years later, it is now possible to begin to review just how far the Pope's Mariology has shaped his pontificate.

Avery Dulles has commented, 'it would be a mistake to think of Karol Wojtyla's attachment to Mary as the fruit of sentimentality... On the contrary, he holds, she occupies an indispensable place in the whole plan of salvation'.[1] Accordingly, the Pope requires of those in the Church who have the task of studying and teaching about Mary 'a method of doctrinal reflection no less rigorous than that used in all theology'.[2] It is through the mirror of his own

---

[1] Avery Dulles, 'Mary at the Dawn of the New Millennium' *America* 178 (1998/3), pp. 8-19, here p. 9.
[2] See his catechesis of December 3, 1996, reported in John Paul II, *Theotókos: Woman, Mother, Disciple* (Boston: Pauline, 2000), p. 54.

Mariology, the fruit of years of his doctrinal reflection, that he has contemplated Jesus, the Church, the human person, history and the world.

In this chapter, after an introductory overview, I shall trace firstly the roots of John Paul's Mariology, then the trunk, as it were, in other words its main elements. This will be followed by a glimpse at the foliage of this Mariology evident in many features of his missionary style and emphases.

THE MARIAN POPE'S TRACK RECORD

Even at a first glance, the Pope's track record in things Marian is impressive. Since taking office at a time when Marian devotion was 'at its lowest ebb since the Enlightenment',[3] he has delivered a staggering number of Marian sermons, prayers, weekly Angelus messages and encyclicals, not to mention a wide range of entrustments and consecrations to Mary (two solemn and official consecrations of the world to Mary on May 13, 1982 and March 25, 1984).

All of his encyclicals and nearly all of his major talks as well as countless minor addresses and letters contain an invocation of Mary or at least a brief and incisive exhortation about her. On his pastoral visits, he regularly consecrates the nation he is visiting to Mary and often takes in a pilgrimage to the chief Marian shrine of the country visited.

As he entered the tenth year of his pontificate, he cast the spotlight once again on Mariology both by producing two encyclical letters, *Redemptoris mater* (25 March 1987)

---

[3] Edward D. O'Connor, 'The Roots of Pope John Paul II's Devotion to Mary' *Marian Studies* 39 (1988), pp.78-114, here p.81.

and *Mulieris dignitatem* (15 August, 1988), and proclaiming a Marian year.

In the mid-1990s Mariology was again to the fore in his *Letter to Women* (29 June, 1995) and the 70 weekly audiences dedicated specifically to a teaching on a Marian theme (September 1995 - November 1997). Most recently, as he entered the year leading up to his twenty-fifth anniversary as Pope, he has presented to the Church an Apostolic Letter on the Rosary, *Rosarium viriginis mariae* (October 16, 2002).[4] The novelty of this letter is, of course, the addition of five new 'mysteries of light' to the traditional mysteries of joy, sorrow and glory contemplated in the Rosary. To be recited on Thursday (Saturday now being dedicated to the Joyful mysteries), these new mysteries (The Baptism of Our Lord; The Wedding Feast of Cana; The Preaching of the Kingdom and Conversion; The Transfiguration and the Institution of the Eucharist) make the Rosary prayer even more a 'compendium of the Gospel'.

TRACING THE ROOTS

The survey just outlined is but an initial sketch. It is necessary now to dig a little deeper and discover the roots of his Marian devotion and theology.

The influence of de Montfort

The beginnings were simple. Love of the image of Our Lady of Perpetual Help in his parish church of Wadowice.

---

[4] All of these documents can be found on the Vatican website, and are available from the CTS, London. For the collection of the seventy general audiences talks on Mary see John Paul II, *Theotókos: Woman, Mother, Disciple*.

Frequent pilgrimages with his parents to the shrine of Kalwaria Zebrzydowska. Visits to the shrine of Jasna Góra with its Black Madonna in Czestochowa, the greatest Marian shrine in Poland (it is here his father took the nine-year-old boy when his mother died). Membership and leadership of a young people's 'Living Rosary' group that prayed for peace and liberation.[5]

But then something of a minor crisis - would Mary detract from the place due to Jesus in his life? It was one of those questions the Holy Spirit puts into a heart because he wants to offer a response. The answer to young Wojtyla's question was discovered in the classic work of Louis-Marie Grignon de Montfort (1673-1716), *True Devotion to the Blessed Virgin Mary*. Reading this book became a truly 'decisive turning-point' in his life. He discovered a Marian devotion that was based completely on Jesus Christ, the Incarnation and Redemption.

De Montfort's work was one of those books that it was not enough to have read. It had to become life. Years later he still remembered carrying it with him for a long time, even at the sodium factory, with the result that its handsome binding became spotted with lime.[6]

From then on, his love of Mary, the Mother of God, sprang from the very heart of the Trinity and Jesus Christ. It deepened into an intellectual vision that would eventually also incorporate his developing insights into the Church and the human person, the world and the course of history.

---

[5] See M. Malinski, *Pope John Paul II* (London: Burns & Oates, 1979), pp. 28-35; George Weigel, *Witness to Hope: The Biography of Pope John Paul II* (London: HarperCollins, 1999), pp. 60-62.
[6] André Frossard, *Be Not Afraid! John Paul II Speaks Out on His Life, His Beliefs and His Inspiring Vision for Humanity* (New York: St. Martin's Press, 1984), p. 125.

In *Crossing the Threshold of Hope*, John Paul II provides an autobiographical summary of this early stage of his life with its lasting effects:

> *Totus Tuus*. This phrase is not only an expression of piety, or simply an expression of devotion. It is more. During the Second World War, while I was employed as a factory worker, I came to be attracted to Marian devotion... Thanks to Saint Louis of Montfort, I came to understand that true devotion to the Mother of God is actually Christocentric, indeed, it is very profoundly rooted in the Mystery of the Blessed Trinity, and the mysteries of the Incarnation and Redemption.... This mature form of devotion to the Mother of God has stayed with me over the years, bearing fruit in the encylicals *Redemptoris mater* and *Mulieris dignitatem*.[7]

The Second Vatican Council

If De Monfort's work launched the young Wojtyla along the path of meditating on the person and role of Mary in the light of Jesus Christ, then Vatican II provided a laboratory of exploration for the new young bishop's theology. Gerald A. McCool comments that Bishop Wojtyla's 'involvement in Vatican II would notably expand his theological horizon'.[8] Indeed, he himself has claimed that his theology was formed at Vatican II.[9]

---

[7] *Crossing the Threshold of Hope* (London: Jonathan Cape, 1994), pp. 212-213.
[8] 'The Theology of John Paul II', in John M McDermott, (ed.), *The Thought of Pope John Paul II* (Rome: PUG, 1993), pp. 29-53, here, p.31.
[9] André Frossard, *Be Not Afraid!*, p. 110.

The Dominican theologian, Yves Congar, who played such an active part in Vatican II, once remarked that 'something happened at the Council and the dominant values in our way of looking at the Church were changed'.[10] It would seem true also for the then Bishop Wojtyla. It has been said that 'Vatican II made him conscious of the "ecclesiotypical" vision of Mary'.[11] In other words, his theological understanding of Mary as model of the Church grew deeper. During one of the sessions of the Council, in September 1964, the recently appointed Archbishop of Krakow affirmed in a written intervention that Mary's motherly role continued in the Mystical Body of Christ.[12]

He was one of the Polish bishops who agreed that the document on Mary should be inserted as a chapter into the document on the Church rather than stand alone as a separate text. However, he wanted this chapter on Mary to be positioned as chapter two rather than as chapter eight of the Dogmatic Constitution on the Church, *Lumen gentium*, because he felt that way it would be more integrated, rather than looking like a corollary added on at the end.[13]

Nevertheless, he was pleased with what eventually became chapter eight, dedicated to Mary, because 'I found reflected in this chapter all my earlier youthful experiences, as well as those special bonds which continue to unite me to the Mother of God in ever new ways'.[14] He was satisfied too when Paul VI at the end of the third session of the

---

[10] See Congar, 'Moving Towards a Pilgrim Church' in A. Stacpoole, (ed.), *Vatican II by those who were there* (London: Geoffrey Chapman, 1986), p. 129.
[11] Edward O'Connor, *'John Paul II's Devotion to Mary'*, p. 112.
[12] See *Acta Synodalia Sacrosancti Concilii Oecumenici Vaticani III-2*, pp. 178-179; Avery Dulles, *'Mary at the Dawn'*, p. 9.
[13] See Edward O'Connor, *'John Paul II's Devotion to Mary'*, p. 88.
[14] *Crossing the Threshold of Hope*, p. 214.

Council, on Nov. 21, 1964, explicitly proclaimed Mary to be Mother of the Church.[15]

A new theological synthesis

The experience of the Council must have been something like a hall of mirrors for the professor-bishop (even after becoming bishop, he continued lecturing). Through his interaction with the many bishops and experts present, especially as he worked very closely on the drafting of the Pastoral Constitution on the Church in the Modern World (*Gaudium et spes*) his speculation with regard to many issues matured. Mariology included. As he himself told later, 'I wrote many parts of books and poems during the sessions of the Council.'[16]

It is known that, as well as the Thomism he so much esteemed, Karol Wojtyla was greatly interested in the phenomenology of Husserl, a philosophical method that he learned about through the writings of the German Catholic philosopher Max Scheler. Now, if it is true that 'for the phenomenologist, the grasp of the truth concerning a particular question only slowly emerges through extensive rumination on the multiple appearances of the question',[17] then it is evident that the event of the Council provided an exciting living space for employing this vital method of enquiry into the link between Mary, Christ, the Church, history and the world.

---

[15] Avery Dulles, '*Mary at the Dawn*', pp. 9-10.
[16] George Weigel, *Witness to Hope*, p. 160ff. See also Michael Walsh, *John Paul II: A Biography* (London: HarperCollins, 1995), p. 27ff.
[17] John. J. Conley, 'Philosophical Foundations of the Thought of John Paul II: A Response' in John M McDermott, (ed.), *The Thought of Pope John Paul II* (Rome: PUG, 1993), pp. 23-28, here p. 25.

So much must have come together in a new synthesis: his early Marian devotion and doctoral studies,[18] his reflection on the link between the notion of the human person as revealed phenomenologically in action and relationship[19] and the emerging focus on the Church as communion, his interest in man in history/culture and the newly rediscovered sense of the continuing Marian presence in the Church and the world.

Mary's faith and her relationship with the Trinity, Marian spirituality and the Church's Marian profile, Mary as model of the human person as gift of self and Mary's motherly care for humanity are all themes that must have resonated deeply within him during the deliberations at the Council. They are themes that run throughout his Papal teaching. Little wonder that in his encyclical explicitly dedicated to Mary, *Redemptoris mater*, he cites the Council over 100 times. And yet, as Cardinal Ratzinger, Hans Urs von Balthasar and others have pointed out, it is also true to say that he takes the Council's teaching a few steps further than what we find expressed in its documents.[20]

EXAMINING THE TRUNK: THE MAIN ELEMENTS OF JOHN PAUL II'S MARIOLOGY

Any brief exposition of the main outlines of John Paul II's Mariology is bound to be extremely limited because, as is commonly known, 'throughout his pontificate,

---

[18] He had written a doctoral thesis at the Angelicum, the Dominicans' university in Rome, under the direction of Réginald Garrigou-Lagrange, on the theme *Faith According to Saint John of the Cross* (San Francisco: Ignatius, 1981).

[19] See John McNerney, *Footbridge towards the Other: An introduction to the philosophy and poetry of John Paul II* (London: T&T Clark, 2003).

[20] See Hans Urs von Balthasar and Joseph Cardinal Ratzinger, *Mary: God's Yes to Man*, (San Francisco: Ignatius, 1988). See also Betrand Budy's preface to the work of Antoine Nachef, *Mary's Pope: John Paul II, Mary and the Church since Vatican II* (Franklin, Wisconsin: Sheed & Ward, 2000), pp. xi-xii.

Pope John Paul II returns again and again to the same concepts, but he analyses them from many different points of view and in relation to many other theological disciplines'.[21] For the purposes of exposition, however, we will divide our overview into three sections: Mary and Jesus Christ; Mary and the Church; Mary, Mother of God and the History of Humanity.

Mary and Jesus Christ: Mary's faith

John Paul II has made his own the twentieth-century theology's rediscovery of the *history* of salvation. He reviews how Mary is at the heart of this history. He does so by reading the Bible as a totality and tracing how the female line of this history leads to Mary.[22]

Mary, *The* Woman, is pre-announced by the words of the 'First Gospel' found in the Book of Genesis (*Gen* 3:15) and shown in eschatological perspective as the 'woman clothed in sun' in the Book of Revelation (12:1). Esteeming Mary's Jewishness, John Paul II refers to her as the virgin 'Daughter of Sion'.

His reflection leads him, of course, to the high point of God's self-communication: Jesus Christ. Mary is central to this event. It is thanks to her that the new and eternal covenant between God and humankind is established.[23] Her 'yes' at the Annunciation when the Holy Spirit came upon her is decisive. It occurs at the 'fullness of time' (*Gal* 4:4), that particular intersection of time and eternity, that fascinates John Paul II.[24]

---

[21] See Antoine Nachef, *Mary's Pope: John Paul II*, p. 11.
[22] See for instance, The Apostolic Letter on the Dignity of Women, *Mulieris dignitatem*, (15 August, 1988), 3, 11, 30.
[23] *Mulieris dignitatem*, 11.
[24] Encyclical Letter on the Blessed Virgin Mary in the Life of the Pilgrim Church, *Redemptoris mater*, (25 March 1987), 1. Also, *Tertio millennio adveniente*, and *Fides et ratio*.

In one of those particular emphases that he brings to bear, John Paul underlines the link between Mary and the Holy Spirit not only at the Annunciation (*Lk* 1:35) but throughout her life. One indication of the importance he ascribes to this is the fact that he mentions this bond over 40 times in *Redemptoris mater.*[25]

The Pope focuses particularly on Mary's faith, the 'yes' to God that she uttered in the power of the Holy Spirit throughout her life. Repeatedly in his teaching John Paul echoes Elizabeth's words: 'Blessed is she who believed' (*Lk* 1:45).

Commenting on the prominent place given to Mary's faith in the encyclical *Redemptoris mater*, von Balthasar remarks: 'Perhaps never before in Mariology has this been done with such decisiveness'.[26] Ratzinger adds the encyclical 'turns into a catechesis about faith.'.[27]

Of course, focus on Mary's faith is not new. We can go right back through the centuries to the famous saying of Irenaeus and other Church Fathers: 'The knot of Eve's disobedience was untied by Mary's obedience'.[28] But John Paul II sings new notes in the centuries-old melody. He underscores the receptive and responsible, vibrant and active, free and feminine aspects of Mary's 'yes'. She responded 'with all her human and feminine 'I''.[29] The Pope also develops the parallel with Eve in terms of her being 'the mother of all living' (*Gen* 3:20).

---

[25] See also the Encyclical Letter On the Holy Spirit in the Life of the Church and the World, *Dominum et vivificantem* (18 May, 1986), 49, 51, 66.
[26] See *Mary: God's Yes to Man*, p. 165.
[27] See *Mary: God's Yes to Man*, p. 25.
[28] *Adversus Haereses III*, 222, 4: *S. Ch*. 211, 438-444.
[29] *Redemptoris mater*, 13.

Stefano De Fiores, the renowned Italian Mariologist, points out that the way John Paul II highlights Mary's faith meets the dilemma of today's Mariology that finds itself between the Scylla of the feminist demand to recognise Mary as a centre of decision and responsibility, and the Charybdis of the Protestant concern to depict Mary as subordinate to Christ the one Mediator.[30]

He does so by reflecting on Mary's 'pilgrimage of faith' as the 'first disciple of her Son'.[31] Her special position did not exempt her from travelling the ups and downs of the spiritual journey of discipleship. John Paul proposes the relevancy of the 'Way of Mary' for all who want to follow Jesus.[32] In describing this journey of faith he avoids a Mariological monophysism by emphasising Mary's humanity.[33]

Mary and the Church: Mary's nuptial identity

John Paul has written that unless one looks to Mary 'it is impossible to understand the mystery of the Church, her reality, her essential vitality'.[34] As he puts it, her faith, her 'yes' to God has entered into 'the very heart' of Christ's fullness.[35] In God's plan, she who accompanied the whole of Jesus' mission was to be the pre-eminent member and model of the Church.

---

[30] Stefano De Fiores, *Maria nella Teologia Contemporanea* (Rome: Centro Mariano Monfortano, 1991), pp. 657-568.
[31] *Redemptoris mater*, Part I, especially n. 20.
[32] See John Paul II's Apostolic Letter on the Rosary, *Rosarium virginis mariae* (16 October, 2002), 24.
[33] De Fiores, *Maria*, p. 568.
[34] *Mulieris dignitatem*, 22.
[35] *Redemptoris mater*, 36.

In drawing an analogy between Christ's Incarnation by the power of the Spirit at the Annunciation, and the birth of the Church in the Upper Room at Pentecost, John Paul II highlights how Mary links both moments.[36] It is through the power of the Holy Spirit that she has been given a pivotal role in the new community born out of Jesus' death and resurrection.

A key text that guides John Paul along his line of meditation is Ephesians 5:25-32, with its image of Christ the Bridegroom and the Church as Bride. As the unique witness to Jesus, and free from sin (the Immaculate Conception), Mary carries out a representative role on our behalf by perfectly accompanying Jesus' work of redemption. She is the 'bride' both born out of, and responding to, Jesus, the Bridegroom's, redemptive love. Her perfect 'yes' is God's gift to humanity, the fruit of the Son of God's death and resurrection, and yet also the pre-condition of his Incarnation and mission.

Mary, therefore, 'precedes' the Church, the Bride of Christ, in the perfection of holiness and love. Her 'yes' includes all our imperfect 'yes-es'. In its deepest reality the Church is a pilgrim people echoing Mary's 'yes' to the Word who became flesh and died for us. Just as Mary was transparent to Christ, so too the Church, as a communion of love among its members is *in, with* and *like* Mary, a Bride transparent to Jesus Christ, the Bridegroom, the One Mediator between humankind and God. That is why John Paul proposes a Marian spirituality that centres on imitation of her 'yes' to God.[37]

---

[36] *Redemptoris mater*, 24.
[37] *Redemptoris mater*, 48.

This topic of the link between Mary and the Church's bridal identity has to be understood together with John Paul's Christian notion of the human person. In reading the biblical account of creation in the light of Jesus Christ's new commandment of love, John Paul II describes how human beings have been created in the image of the Trinity as a gift to one another.[38] This giftedness is seen especially in the mutual gift of partners in marriage. But each person, be they single or married, is called to realise their 'nuptial' identity through the gift of their whole life to God and to others.

Mary is the paradigm of this nuptial dimension of being human. She shows us what it means to say that our human vocation is to 'receive love, in order to love in return'.[39] She exemplifies it in accompanying Jesus' mission from the very beginning. She continues now her 'bridal' co-operation with the Risen Christ in his continuing mission through the Church in the world. It is a theme upon which John Paul elaborates more than did the Second Vatican Council. It leads us directly to the theme of Mary's maternity.

Mary, Mother of God and the history of humanity: Mary's maternal mediation

Among the many biblical meditations offered by the Pope, one topic comes up repeatedly: Mary's experience at the foot of the Cross (*Jn* 19:25). It is the moment when she who had co-operated all the way along with Jesus's mission now shares in the shocking mystery of his self-emptying.

---

[38] See *Gaudium et spes*, 22 and 24 repeatedly quoted by John Paul II throughout his Pontificate.
[39] *Mulieris dignitatem*, 29.

'This is perhaps the deepest *kenosis* of faith in human history'.[40] But it is at this moment that the dying Jesus entrusts Mary to John and John (representing humanity) to Mary, thus bestowing upon her a new, expanded and universal motherhood (*Jn* 19:25-27).[41]

Mary's maternity is perhaps *the* major theme in John Paul's teaching. While the Second Vatican Council spoke of Mary as model of the Church, John Paul II also emphasises how 'Mary, herself, then, through her own everlasting motherhood "cooperates in the birth and development of the sons and daughters of Mother Church"'.[42] Cardinal Ratzinger believes the Pope deepens the Council's teaching on this topic, providing more substance for study and devotion.[43]

John Paul teaches and writes of Mary's maternal 'mediation'. It is a carefully chosen term, to be distinguished from the term 'mediatrix'. He develops his reflection on Mary's maternal mediation by taking his lead from the definition of Mary as *Theotókos*, the bearer or mother of God, found in the Council of Ephesus (431 AD). It is Mary's divine motherhood that provides the source of her unique maternal mediation.[44] While always viewing Jesus Christ as the sole mediator, the Pope notes that it is an inclusive mediation, allowing for forms of participation.

If, for the Apostle Paul, 'we are God's fellow worker' (*1 Cor* 3:9), then none more so than the woman who co-operated with Christ's mission from its very beginning. She perfectly heard, kept and put into practice Jesus' word (see *Lk* 11:28 and

---

[40] *Redemptoris mater*, 18.
[41] *Redemptoris mater*, 23.
[42] *Redemptoris mater*, 44. See Von Balthasar, *Mary: God's Yes to Man*, p. 172.
[43] Ratzinger, *Mary: God's yes to Man*, p. 31.
[44] Audience', 9 April 1997. See John Paul II, *Theotókos*, pp. 185-187.

Lk 8:20f) and at the end of her life was assumed into heaven.

Now, as the supreme 'witness to the new "beginning" and the "new creation"' (*cf. 2 Cor* 5:17) of the world in Jesus Christ,[45] Mary continues her unique role of maternal mediation in the Church and in the history of humankind. It is totally related to Christ, the Son of God, who is always born anew into this world. John Paul views the episode at Cana as offering us a first announcement of Mary's maternal meditation (*Jn* 2:1-11). As presented in John's Gospel, Mary has great 'solicitude for human beings' and comes to them 'in the wide variety of their wants and needs'.[46] Her maternal mediation is one of intercession for humanity.

In commenting on this maternal mediation, John Paul often makes reference to the Book of Revelation that presents Mary under the Sign of the Woman (*Rev* 12). Mary is the Woman who 'reigns' because she serves. Her service takes the shape of a maternal mediation that extends throughout the history of the Church and the world in the struggle between good and evil.[47]

It has been commented that John Paul's reflections on the Book of Revelation's vision of the Woman, found in chapter VIII of *Mulieris dignitatem*, offer a new perspective for Catholic theology, resonating with a theme dear to oriental theology (Bulgakov for example), namely, the deep relationship between Mary and creation, between Mary and the cosmos in its original vocation, fulfilled in the grace of redemption and divinisation.[48]

---

[45] *Mulieris dignitatem*, 11.
[46] *Redemptoris mater*, 21.
[47] *Redemptoris mater*, 24 and 47 and *Mulieris dignitatem*, 5.
[48] Piero Coda 'Teologia e antropologia nella 'Mulieris dignitatem' *Nuova Umanità* 11 (1989) 9-29, here p. 29.

LOOKING AT THE FOLIAGE:
EXPRESSIONS OF JOHN PAUL II'S MARIOLOGY

In the last section of this chapter, we want to observe the foliage, as it were, of John Paul II's Mariology. How has it impacted concretely on his pastoral mission, his view of the Church and outreach to the world? What concrete expressions of his Mariology can we detect?

A significant starting point is an address he delivered to the Roman Curia just a few days before Christmas 1987. In it, he referred to a novel way of looking at the Church. He spoke of the Church's two profiles - the Marian ('subjective' holiness, charisms and authentic witness to the Gospel in everyday life) and the Petrine ('objective' means of sanctification such as the sacraments effected by bishops and priests). He described how all that goes on in the life of the Church revolves around these two profiles. Future years may credit him with having directed our attention to a rediscovery and a new appreciation of the Marian dimension as a key aspect of the Church:

> This Marian profile is also - even perhaps more so - fundamental and characteristic for the Church as is the apostolic and Petrine profile to which it is profoundly united.... The Church lives on this authentic 'Marian profile', this 'Marian dimension'... The Marian dimension of the Church is antecedent to that of the Petrine... Mary...precedes all others, including obviously Peter himself and the Apostles... The link between the two profiles of the Church, the Marian and the Petrine, is profound and complementary. This is so even though the Marian profile is anterior (to that of the Petrine) not

only in the plan of God but also in time, as well as being supreme and pre-eminent, the richer in personal and communitarian implications....[49]

Some months later, he returned to this theme in his apostolic letter, *Mulieris dignitatem*.[50] In his 1995 letter to priests for Holy Thursday, he recommended they re-read *Mulieris dignitatem* and also, in 1995, he wrote on this theme in his *Letter to Women*. In 1998, during a catechesis on the signs of hope in the Church, he commented, 'At the dawn of the new millennium, we notice with joy the emergence of the Marian profile of the Church that summarises the deepest contents of the Conciliar renewal'.[51]

It seems to the present writer that John Paul II's appreciation of the Church's Marian profile explains much of his teaching on lay people in the Church, his encouragement of the new ecclesial movements, his promotion of the dignity of women in the Church and the world, his view on ecumenism, and his enormous outreach to the world.

Lay people in the Church

George Weigel has written that the Pope's 'new evangelisation' of the twenty-first century demands a Church that has transcended clericalism.[52] This explains why a major aim of his pontificate has been 'to emphasise forcefully the priestly, prophetic and kingly

---

[49] See *L'Osservatore Romano* [English Edition], 11 January 1988, pp. 6-8.
[50] See *Mulieris dignitatem*, 27, fn. 55.
[51] 23 November 1998. *L'Osservatore Romano* [English Edition], 2 December 1998. p.19.
[52] Weigel, *Witness to Hope*, p. 554.

dignity of the entire People of God.'[53] It is precisely the bi-polarity of the Marian and Petrine profiles of the Church that provides the Pope with a vibrant perspective of the role of laity.

For him, the Church is not a clerical preserve in which lay people help or get involved. That smacks of a clericalisation of the laity. Instead, recognition of the dynamic Marian profile of the Church points to a vibrant lay vocation, that of bringing Christ into the world.

With Mary as their model, the lay faithful reach holiness *through* rather than in spite of their involvement in business, politics, the media, art etc. The Pope's Mariology leads him to see lay people as expressing the Church as she proclaims the Kingdom of God in the world with the *Magnificat* as their *Magna Carta*.[54]

New ecclesial movements

The emergence of new ecclesial movements, such as *Charismatic Renewal*, *Communion and Liberation*, *Cursillo*, *Faith and Light*, *Focolare*, *L'Arche*, *Sant'Egidio* and *Youth 2000*, is a feature of the Church's life that the Pope reads in terms of the Marian profile.[55]

Taking his lead from Vatican II, the Pope views the Movements as an expression of the Church's charismatic dimension which is co-essential with the institutional aspect. Influenced possibly also by von Balthasar, he views this

---

[53] See John Paul II, Post-Synodal Apostolic Exhortation, *Christifideles laici*, (30 December, 1988), 14.
[54] See *Christifideles laici*, 64.
[55] On the movements, see Ian Ker, 'Are the new movements the true expression of Vatican II?' *Catholic Herald* (10 September 1999).

charism-institution polarity within the interplay between the Marian-Petrine profiles.[56] Not surprisingly. St. Louis Marie Grignon de Montfort said that two alone are capable of giving birth together, in synergy, to the Son of God in the flesh and, in him, to us too as sons and daughters of the Father - namely, the Holy Spirit and Mary. Since the ecclesial movements are an authentic gift of the Spirit, it follows they are bound also to Mary, the woman who links the Annunciation and Pentecost descents of the Spirit.

Women in the Church

As we have seen above, in his encyclical letter on the dignity of women, John Paul II presents the Marian profile as the key to a new appreciation of women in the Church. Indeed, he sees a certain priority in what he calls the 'feminine genius' summarised in Mary. He also writes of the 'prophetic characteristic of woman in her femininity'.[57]

In Paris in 1980 he commented: 'Just as it is true that the Church at a hierarchical level is guided by the successors of the apostles and therefore by men, it is even truer that in a charismatic sense, it is women as well as men who guide it, and perhaps even more so'.[58]

In an Angelus address delivered on 3 September 1995, Pope John Paul II referred again to Mary as the model of the Church and ideal of femininity, and made a plea for

---

[56] For development of this theme see David Schindler 'Institution and Charism' and Piero Coda 'The Ecclesial Movements, Gift of the Spirit: A Theological Reflection' in Pontifical Council for the Laity, *Movements in the Church* (Vatican, 1999), pp.53-76 and 77-105.

[57] *Mulieris dignitatem*, 30.

[58] See *Insegnamenti di Giovanni Paolo II*, III/1 (Vatican: 1980), p. 1628.

the Christian community to be more faithful to God's plan, also for the participation of women in the Church. He referred to proposition 47 of the 1987 Synod of the Laity, asking that 'without discrimination women should be participants in the life of the Church and also in consultation and the process of coming to decisions'.[59] He went on to list the ways already open for this and then concluded: 'Who can imagine the great advantages to pastoral care and the new beauty that the Church's face will assume, when the feminine genius is fully involved in various areas of her life?'.[60]

Chiara Lubich, foundress of the *Focolare Movement*, tells of how she asked the Pope if in the future the president of the *Focolare* (with its variety of vocations including lay people, consecrated men and women, priests, religious and bishops) should always be a woman. He replied with enthusiasm 'And why not? On the contrary'. He went on to explain his vision of the Marian profile of the Church as the all-embracing dimension of the Church.[61]

Ecumenical and inter-religious dialogue

While John Paul recognises that the doctrine about Mary is one of the areas where disagreement still exists in the ecumenical movement, nevertheless it could be argued that also in the field of ecumenism his Mariology plays an important part.

His Mariology is not one that could be classified as a 'privilege' Mariology in the sense of underlining Mary's

---

[59] See also *Christifideles laici*, 51.
[60] See *L'Osservatore Romano* [English Edition], 3 September 1995.
[61] See Franca Zambonini, *Chiara Lubich: A Life for Unity* (New City: London, 1992), pp.142ff and Jim Gallagher, *A Woman's Work* (London: HarperCollins, 1997), pp.202ff.

titles and privileges unilaterally.[62] Nevertheless, he does entrust the cause of unity among Christians to Mary, whom Augustine called 'the Mother of unity'.[63] And it has been said that his focus on Mary's faith is like a 'passionate dialogue with Martin Luther'.[64]

There is, however, a more indirect way his Mariology shapes his views on ecumenism. He constantly refers to the primacy of spiritual ecumenism and holiness. Could this, too, not be because of his theological reflection on Mary, Jesus's first disciple, the woman who shows the primacy of holiness in the Church? While there may be difficulties in the more institutional inter-relationship of the churches, it would seem that the Pope encourages developments at the level of the Church's Marian profile:

> By a more profound study of both Mary and the Church, clarifying each by the light of the other, Christians...will be able to go forward... Mary...is to lead them to the unity which is willed by their one Lord and so much desired by those who are attentively listening to what 'the Spirit is saying to the Churches' today (*Rev* 2:7, 11,17).[65]

In terms of the inter-religious dialogue in which the Catholic Church is engaged and to which he personally has contributed so much, it could be said that his Mariology plays its part. In one of his encyclicals we read that it is

---

[62] He has not proceeded with proclaiming Marian titles such as 'coredemptrix', 'mediatrix of all graces' and 'advocate of the people of God' because of ecumenical considerations. See Dulles, *'Mary at the Dawn'*, pp. 10-16.

[63] *Sermo* 192, 2: PL 38, 1013.

[64] See Joseph Cardinal Ratzinger and Hans Urs von Balthasar, *Mary: God's Yes to Man* (San Francisco: Ignatius, 1988), p. 168. On the ecumenical theme see also Frederick M. Jelly, 'Ecumenical Aspects of *Redemptoris Mater*' 39 (1988) *Marian Studies*, pp. 115-129

[65] *Redemptoris mater*, 30.

necessary to understand Mary 'from the point of view of man's spiritual history, understood in the widest possible sense, and as this history is expressed through the different world religions'.[66]

Outreach to the world

One of the outstanding features of John Paul II's pontificate has been his constant, indefatigable outreach to individuals and peoples, nations and ethnical groups, communities and institutions - in a word, his pastoral outreach to the world. Clearly this, too, is linked with his Mariology:

> Since 'the Church is in Christ as a sacrament...of the intimate union with God and of the unity of the whole human race' (*Lumen gentium*, 1), the special presence of the Mother of God in the mystery of the Church makes us think of the exceptional link between this 'woman' and the whole human family.[67]

As 'the representative and the archetype of the whole human race',[68] Mary, the mother of humanity, 'knows well the needs and aspirations of humanity'.[69] Regarding Mary as the most perfect image of the freedom and liberation of humanity and the universe,[70] John Paul engages actively in the events of today's world. He does so in the conviction that the Church 'sees Mary deeply rooted in humanity's

---

[66] *Mulieris dignitatem*, 3
[67] *Mulieris dignitatem*, n.2
[68] *Mulieris dignitatem*, n. 4
[69] See the General Audience, November 12, 1997 in *Theotókos*, p. 260.
[70] *Redemptoris mater*, 37.

history... She sees Mary maternally present and sharing in the many complicated problems which today beset the lives of individuals, families and nations; she sees her helping the Christian people in the constant struggle between good and evil, to ensure that it 'does not fall', or, if it has fallen, that it 'rises again'.[71] Most recently, we see this perspective in his exhortation on the Church in Europe.[72]

CONCLUSION

In John's Gospel we read that at the foot of the Cross, after Jesus entrusted John to Mary and Mary to John, 'the disciple took her to his home' (*Jn* 19:27). John Paul II reads this episode as an invitation to admit Mary into our innermost regions, so that Christ might be born, again and again, within us. It is his personal response to this invitation that has been the most significant factor in his pontificate.

As a young man he took part in a 'living rosary' group that prayed for peace and liberation. Since then he has participated in numerous initiatives that promote the good. He has sought to lead the Church into the New Evangelisation needed for a new millennium. Now, with the arrival of his twenty-fifth anniversary as Pope, he has returned to the theme of Mary once again by publishing an apostolic letter on the Rosary.

On the other hand, he clearly wants to promote this Christo-centric prayer as a contribution towards world peace and harmony in family life. But perhaps this simple letter also wants to reveal that, yes indeed, Mariology has been a key reference point throughout these twenty five years.

---

[71] *Redemptoris mater*, 52.
[72] See John Paul II, Post-Synodal Apostolic Exhortation, *Ecclesia in europa*, 28 June 2003, 122-125.

For he sees in Mary so much of the Christian humanism
that needs now to be promoted in the third millennium:

> Mary means, in a sense, a going beyond the limit spoken
> of in the Book of Genesis (3:16) and a return to that
> 'beginning' in which one finds the 'woman' as she was
> intended to be in creation, and therefore in the eternal
> mind of God: in the bosom of the Most Holy Trinity.[73]

For him, the Trinity is not just a doctrine, but a reality
that we share in and can live on earth, just as Mary did. The
'Marian service' he wants to offer to the world is to
promote the spirit of communion and universal fraternity
that flows from the life of mutual love that Jesus brought
on earth, a life that reflects the life of the Trinity.[74] He
believes it is crucial at this moment of history.

His more than 100 pastoral journeys are eloquent
testimony to what could be called a maternal contribution
that he wants to make, as he vigorously defends life and
promotes justice, peace and solidarity.

For John Paul II, the *'totus tuus'* he addresses to Mary is
not just a figure of speech. It is a code by which he lives.
I conclude this chapter, therefore, by recalling a personal
memory. On May 13, 1991, together with about 40 others,
I attended the Pope's early morning Mass. He was due to
go, later that day, to Fatima in thanksgiving, 10 years after
the assassination attempt on his life. After Mass, he greeted
each one of us personally, without any trace of being in a
rush. He even stopped for a group photograph. Jokingly,

---

[73] *Mulieris dignitatem*, 11.
[74] See the Second Vatican Council's document on the Church in the Modern World, *Gaudium et spes*, 22 and 24.

he concluded our time together, saying, 'and now it's time for breakfast!'. Later that day, I turned on the television and saw him in Fatima with one million pilgrims. The thought occurred to me that whether it was greeting us in the morning, going for breakfast, or being with a million pilgrims, what mattered for John Paul II was to live the present moment well, each present moment.

Many years before he would have read de Montfort's invitation to cast ourselves into the 'mould' of Mary as a simpler way of progressing in our spiritual life. Having cast himself into this mould, John Paul II has sought simply to love and live each present moment entrusting himself to Mary.

The Almighty has, indeed, done great things.

V

RECOGNISING THE ROSE: JOHN PAUL II

AND THE CAUSES OF THE SAINTS

John Saward

In form, then, of a snow-white rose
There shone before me the saintly host
That with His blood Christ made His spouse.[1]

D ante saw the saints in paradise in the form of a radiant
rose. While still in mortal flesh, he had the privilege of
glimpsing the beauty of the heavenly Church, the glorious
bride whose members wear robes made white by the blood
of the lamb (*cf Apoc* 7: 14). When the Pope canonizes saints,
he makes no claim to see what Dante saw. He is the supreme
pastor of the earthly Church, which walks by faith not sight
(*cf 2 Cor* 5: 7). The bride of Christ here below does not look
upon the faces of those high above who behold the face of
God, but she does know the names of the greatest of them
and begs them unceasingly to help her. 'In the first place',[2]

---

[1] *Paradiso* 31, 1 - 3.
[2] *Cf* the Roman Canon.

she calls upon the ever-virgin Mother of God, then St John the Baptist and St Joseph, the apostles and the martyrs, and finally all whose heroic sanctity she has affirmed by solemn decree. Even in this life, the Church can recognize a small part of the celestial rose; she is a pilgrim, but not a complete stranger, to the Jerusalem on high. Day by day, the king of heaven, escorted by the angels, becomes present on her altars. In exile, as in the fatherland, there is but one bride wedded to one bridegroom, the incarnate Son of the Father, and he, by the working of the Holy Spirit, leads her into all the truth (*cf Jn* 16: 13), including the truth about the saints. Yes, the Holy Spirit gives the Church militant a knowledge, albeit limited, of the Church triumphant, and enables her, through the Roman Pontiff, to declare a certain soul to be reigning with Christ in glory, and to be worthy of the honour that is due to the saints. This declaration, which we call 'canonization',[3] is a definitive and indeed infallible act. When the Church holds up one of the faithful departed for our veneration, she does not and cannot err.[4] How monstrous it would be if she were to commend as an example of sanctity someone whose soul, unbeknown to her, was suffering eternal torment for unrepented sin! Such a monstrosity has

---

[3] 'The Apostolic See, accepting the signs and voice of the Lord with the greatest awe amd docility, from time immemorial, for the weighty task of teaching, sanctifying, and governing the People of God, offers - for the imitation, veneration, and invocation of the faithful - men and women outstanding for the splendour of charity and all the other evangelical virtues, and, having conducted the necessary scrutiny, declares by a solemn act of canonization that they are saints' (Pope John Paul II, *Divinus perfectionis magister*, 1).

[4] 'The honour we show the saints is a certain profession of faith by which we believe in their glory, and it is to be piously believed that even in this judgement of the Church is not able to err' (St Thomas, *Quaestiones quodlibetales* 9, q. 8, a. 16, ad 2). The Pope does not act infallibly when he beatifies. Beatification is only the permission granted for the veneration of a holy person in a particular place or community, whereas canonization is a definitive act, the imposing of a precept of veneration upon all the faithful. Beatification is a preparation for the definitive act of canonization, and therefore engages the Pope's apostolic authority at a lower level.

never occurred, nor can it. Canonization is a solemn act pertaining to faith and morals, and so, in making it, the Church is preserved from error by Christ her head. With divinely assured perception, she can recognize the rose, discern the fragrance of grace in the lives of the saints on earth, and be confident about the brilliance of the glory that their souls now enjoy in heaven.

The process of saint-making: recognizing the radiance

The present Holy Father has recognized the radiance of the rose in a great number of souls. It is very likely that he has 'made'[5] more saints than any of his predecessors, indeed more than all of his predecessors put together. The list includes some of the best loved of the holy persons of modern times, such as St Maximilian Kolbe and St Padre Pio.[6] The numbers are large because the Pope has beatified whole battalions of martyrs, such as the victims of the French Revolution and Spanish Civil War, as well as eighty-five of our own countrymen who died for the true faith in penal times. Martyrs of the twentieth century are particularly prominent among the new entries in the catalogue of sainthood. 'In our own century', says the Holy Father, 'the martyrs have returned, many of them nameless, unknown soldiers, as it were, of God's great cause'.[7] The

---

[5] Strictly speaking, of course, it is God, not the Pope, who makes the saints by his grace: the Triune God alone is the principal efficient cause of the sanctity of the saints. The Pope merely proclaims that sanctity by an ecclesiastical decree. However, there is an important sense in which the Holy Father can and does serve as an instrumental cause of the sanctity of the faithful, namely, by his teaching on Christian faith and morality: he gives us the truth according to which the holy life is to be lived. And, of course, the Bishop of Rome, like every other bishop and priest, gives us the grace that makes us holy in the Sacraments of the Church.
[6] Mother Teresa of Calcutta will be declared 'Blessed' in October 2003.
[7] *Tertio millennio adveniente*, 37.

Pope is convinced that the blood of the martyrs is the seed of Christians, and that now, as in the past, it will bring forth the harvest of a Christendom renewed. The newly canonized and beatified include all sorts and conditions of Catholics - male and female, young and old, learned and unlettered, clerical and lay, virgins and married couples, contemplatives of the cloister and apostles of the street. Perhaps the most remarkable of the laypersons raised to the honour of the altars are the visionaries of Fatima, Blessed Francisco and Jacinta, the youngest children, apart from the martyrs, ever to be declared blessed by the Church. This act of John Paul II confirms the prophecy of his predecessor St Pius X when he lowered the age for First Holy Communion: 'There will be saints among the children!'

Pope John Paul wants the captivating beauty of holiness, the radiance of the rose, to shine anew upon the minds and hearts of the faithful. His goal is to encourage each of us to take up afresh the call to holiness, which, as he says, is 'rooted in Baptism': we must become what we are by the grace of our baptism.[8] This proclamation of the successor of St Peter echoes the exhortation of St Paul. The Apostle frequently addresses the Christians to whom he writes as 'saints', but at the same time he urges them to live saintly lives: they are holy, and yet they have to become holy (*cf 1 Cor* 1: 2; *Eph* 1: 1; 5: 3). To make sense of what the Apostle and the Pope are saying, let us remind ourselves of the effects of holy Baptism. Consider, for example, a newly christened baby. He is, in one way, a little saint. If he were to die in infancy, he would go straight to heaven. Christ the

---

[8] *Christifideles laici*, 16.

Saviour has washed original sin from his soul and imprinted his seal, his indelible character, upon him.[9] The new little Christian is aglow with the sanctifying grace that makes him a sharer in the life of the blessed Trinity. He is an adopted child of the Father, a member of the Son, a temple of the Holy Spirit, a partaker of the divine nature. Although he cannot yet make free acts of faith, hope, and charity, the theological virtues exist as habits in the powers of his soul. The gifts of the Holy Spirit are likewise installed, like sails in a newly fitted ship, ready and waiting to catch the wind of divine inspirations.[10] Yes, the baptized baby is a saint - for the time being. Soon, with the dawning of reason and the awakening of concupiscence, a spiritual battle will begin. He will be exposed to the attacks of the world, the flesh, and the devil. He is holy, but he must remain holy and grow in holiness. The young Christian must exercise the virtues, theological and moral, that have been infused into his soul with baptismal grace. He must allow the Holy Spirit by his gifts to perfect his practice of the virtues,[11] and to bring forth those special acts of Christian virtue which the Apostle calls the 'fruits of the Spirit'.[12] Our Lord wants to draw the baptized into ever closer friendship with himself and the Father in the unity of the Holy Spirit.[13] To that end all the

---

[9] Cf The Catechism of the Catholic Church 1250, 1263, 1272.
[10] Cf CCC 1266.
[11] Cf ibid., 1831.
[12] Cf ibid., 1832.
[13] My argument passes from the call to holiness to the call to the mystical life. This transition is in line with the *Catechism*, which speaks of a general (presumably remote) call to mystical union with the Trinity when it is discussing 'Christian holiness': 'Spiritual progress tends towards ever more intimate union with Christ. This union is called "mystical" because it participates in the mystery of Christ through the sacraments - "the holy mysteries" - and, in him, in the mystery of the Holy Trinity. *God calls us all to this intimate union with him, even if the special graces or extraordinary signs of this mystical life are granted only to some for the sake of manifesting the gratuitous gift given to all*' (CCC 2014).

other sacraments are ordered, above all the holy Eucharist, in which the God-Man is really present, offered, and received. The divine bridegroom invites us to a spiritual marriage with himself, but in order to attain that high union the soul must undergo a deep purgation, costly configuration to Christ crucified, harrowing nights of sense and spirit.[14] Then indeed does the Christian become what he is by his baptism. Every living thing seeks and aims at its perfection: the apple tree at its fruit, the rose at its flower. The surging movement of a thing towards a greater wholeness, towards the goods that make it better and more complete - that's life. And that, too, is the Christian life. By the grace of his baptism, the believer is alive with the supernatural life of grace, partaking of the life of the Trinity. That life must grow within him, from purgation and illumination to intimate union, to transformation in the beloved. As the Fathers of the Second Vatican Council put it, we must, with God's help, 'hold on to and perfect in [our] lives the sanctification [we] have received from God'.[15]

We must make a couple of distinctions. First, though the soul's mystical union with the Triune God is the summit of perfection in this world, it is only a foretaste of the final perfection of that union which we hope to enjoy hereafter. The holiness of grace is fulfilled in the holiness of glory: in the beatific vision, the communion of saints, the resurrection of the body, and the life everlasting. Secondly, while sanctifying grace makes the Christian essentially perfect, whole and holy in his being, it is charity that makes

---

[14] *Cf* St John of the Cross, *The Ascent of Mount Carmel*, bk. 2, ch. 7, n. 11.
[15] *Lumen gentium*, 40.

him operatively perfect, whole and holy in his action.[16] The Pope and the Council, in agreement with all of the Church's great Doctors, teach us that the perfection of Christian life, the truly saintly life, consists chiefly in charity, in loving God above all things and our neighbour as ourselves for the love of God. The saints are those who say and mean and live out the words of the act of charity: 'I love you, Jesus, my love above all things'. The holy God is the God of love, the trinitarian God whose innermost life is an eternal communion of consubstantial persons. To be holy is to participate in the holiness of the Trinity and thus in the Trinity's life of love. 'God is love, and he who abides in love abides in God, and God abides in him' (1 *Jn* 4: 16). 'Love', says St Thomas, 'has a transforming power', a transporting power; it carries us away into the heart of the beloved.[17] So it is with the saints' love of Christ: it transports them into his Sacred Heart, where he loves the Father in the fire of the Holy Spirit. We *live* the life of God by love. The civilization of love is not a Utopian dream of the future; it is already a reality in the present, in the communion of the saints in charity.

The Holy Father has said many times that the call to holiness, to the perfect love of God, lies at the centre of the Council's teaching: it is 'an intrinsic and essential aspect' of its doctrine of the Church,[18] the 'basic charge' it has bequeathed to Christ's faithful.

This charge is not a simple moral exhortation but an undeniable requirement arising from the mystery of the

---

[16] *Cf* St Thomas Aquinas, *De veritate* q. 27, a. 2.
[17] *Cf Quaestiones quodlibetales* 3, q. 6, a. 3.
[18] *Novo millennio ineunte*, 30.

Church: she is the choice vine whose branches live and grow with the same holy and life-giving energies that come from Christ; she is the mystical body whose members share in the same life of holiness of the head who is Christ; she is the beloved bride of the Lord Jesus who delivered himself up for her sanctification (*cf. Eph* 5:25ff.). The Spirit that sanctified the human nature of Jesus in Mary's virginal womb (*cf. Lk* 1:35) is the same Spirit that is abiding and working in the Church to communicate to her the holiness of the Son of God made man.[19]

The argument is clear: what Christ is, the Church must also be; but what the Church is, each of her members is called to become.

The purpose of saint-making: reaching the rose

The Holy Father, like his predecessors, beatifies and canonizes for four great reasons. The primary purpose is to give glory to the Holy Trinity and the sacred humanity of the Son, for it is by the Holy Trinity, through the sacred humanity of the Son, that the saints are made saintly: 'By proclaiming and venerating the holiness of her sons and daughters,' says the Pope, 'the Church [gives] supreme honour to God himself; in the martyrs she venerate[s] Christ, who [is] at the origin of their martyrdom and of their holiness.' This truth is beautifully expressed in one of the Prefaces in the Missal: 'Thou art glorified in the assembly of the saints, and in crowning their merits, thou crownest

---

[19] *Christifideles laici* 16.

thine own gifts'. God's supernatural gifts of sanctifying grace and charity are the prerequisite for the meriting of eternal life; the merits of the saints therefore show forth his glory. On the eve of his passion, our Lord imparts the same teaching: 'He who abides in me, and I in him, he it is that bears much fruit, for apart from me you can do nothing... By this my Father is glorified, that you bear much fruit' (*Jn* 15: 8). The fruit of sanctity manifests the glory of the Father, for without the merits of the Son sent in human nature by the Father, and without the grace of the Holy Spirit poured into our hearts by the Father and the Son, we can do nothing of supernatural worth.

The second reason for canonizing the saints is to enable the faithful to venerate them and ask for their prayers. The Holy Father wants us to remember that we live and move and have our being in the great solidarity of the mystical body, to see the Church under the aspect of her sweetest name, the communion of saints. The Council of Trent, summarizing the perennial faith of the Church, teaches us that 'the saints, reigning with Christ, pray to God for [us]', and that 'it is good and useful to invoke them humbly; and to have recourse to their prayers'.[20] Now, if we are to venerate the saints and 'invoke them humbly', we need to know who they are. The Church gives us that knowledge when she raises the servants of God to the honours of the altar.

The third purpose of canonization is to display the loveliness of the Church's holiness and thereby the reasonableness of her faith. The saints are the Church's

---

[20] *Cf* Denzinger-Schönmetzer, *Enchiridion symbolorum*, 1821.

most persuasive apologetic, and their sanctity is what the First Vatican Council calls a 'motive of credibility'.[21] Holiness, in the Pope's words, is 'a message that convinces without the need for words'; it is 'the living reflection of the face of Christ'.[22] Search as we may among the religions of the world, we shall find nothing to compare with the heroic virtues of the saints of the Catholic Church. Hans Urs von Balthasar argued this point very bluntly in the 1970s: 'It never occurred to Indian wisdom in all its sublimity to pick up the dying from the streets of Calcutta. That has now been done by the foolishness of Mother Teresa, who has thus enlightened all the holy gurus as to how and why Christianity is a human religion.'[23] The little Albanian nun, by her mission of charity, proved that Christianity is a human religion, because it is the true religion revealed by God-made-man.

The Church's fourth reason for declaring someone to be a saint is to encourage all her children to take up the call to holiness, to help them reach the rose of heaven. Knowing, as Dante did, that the rose bears petals from every time and place, and from every state of Christian life, the Pope wants to provide us with practical examples and ready helpers for the sanctification of every duty and circumstance of our earthly journey. Many of the saints have acknowledged that they themselves were led to sanctity through reading or hearing about the holy men of the past. Reading the biography of St Antony strengthened

---

[21] Denzinger-Schönmetzer, 3013. In the words of Pope Pius XII, holiness is one of 'the many wonderful, God-given external signs that are sufficient to prove with certitude by the natural light of reason alone the divine origins of the Christian religion' (Denzinger-Schönmetzer, 3876).
[22] *Novo millennio ineunte*, 7.
[23] *New Elucidations*, ET (San Francisco, 1986), p. 86 (translation adapted).

St Augustine's resolve during the final stages of his journey to the truth. His own *Confessions* have likewise been an instrument of conversion for countless Christian souls. When he was convalescing after the battle of Pamplona, St Ignatius of Loyola, lacking any light reading, took up the lives of the saints and began to ask himself: 'What if I should do what St Francis did, what St Dominic did?' Looking back in 2001 on the Jubilee of the previous year, the Holy Father thanked our Lord for the grace of being able to beatify and canonize so many Christians, 'and among them many lay people who attained holiness in the most ordinary circumstances of life.'[24] The Pope said he wanted to refute any suggestion that you can only be holy if you have 'some kind of extraordinary existence'. No, says the Holy Father, 'the ways of holiness are many, according to the vocation of each individual'. Sanctity is the 'high standard of *ordinary* Christian living'.[25] It is through simple fidelity, with the help of grace, to the duties of our state of life, by humbly believing and hoping and loving Jesus in the daily round, that we shall reach the rose and shine with all the saints in glory. The road to the rose is the 'little way'. Even the Queen of All Saints followed her Son by this path, as the youngest of all the Church's Doctors teaches us in one of her poems:

The number of little ones on earth is very great.
They can raise their eyes to you without trembling.
It is the common path, O matchless Mother,

[24] *Ibid*. During the synod on the laity in 1987, he also beatified several lay persons 'new models of holiness and new witnesses of heroic virtue lived in the ordinary everyday circumstances of human existence' (*cf Christifideles laici* 16).
[25] *Novo millennio ineunte*, 31.

That you are pleased to tread so you can guide them to heaven.[26]

Here we see the great blessing of consecration to our Lady as preached by St Louis de Montfort and the Holy Father: it enables us, day by day, to draw upon our Lady's simplicity and purity for the fulfilment of our baptismal vows.

The Holy Father has been particularly keen on providing married couples with models among the saints. 'Precisely because we are convinced of the abundant fruits of holiness in the married state,' said the Pope in his encyclical for the Jubilee, 'we need to find the most appropriate means for discerning [the heroic virtues of the married] and proposing them to the whole Church as a model and encouragement for other Christian spouses.'[27] The Pope has been true to his word. In 1994 he declared the parents of St Thérèse, Louis and Zélie Martin, to be 'venerable'. Among those he has beatified, we should mention Frédéric Ozanam, apologist of Catholic truth and apostle of Christian charity, who was both husband and father; Gianna Beretta Molla, wife, mother, and physician, who at the age of thirty-nine laid down her life for the sake of her unborn child; and Marcel Callo, hero of the Young Christian Workers and model for the engaged, who said that his sufferings in a Nazi concentration camp would purge him of faults that might later hurt the woman he intended to marry. The dying words of Blessed Gianna

---

[26] The poem by St Thérèse of Lisieux, '*Pourquoi je t'aime, ô Marie*'.
[27] *Tertio millennio adveniente*, 37.

reveal the heart of her lay sanctity, of the sanctity of all the saints in every state of Christian life: 'Jesus, I love you, Jesus, I love you'.

Conclusion

No pope has ever canonized Dante, though one pope of the last century, Benedict XV, honoured him with an encyclical on the sixth centenary of his death. We must not make Dante the object of veneration as a saint, but we ought to admire his own example of veneration of the saints. *The Divine Comedy* is built upon the belief that the head of the mystical body bestows his grace through the intercession of the saints, those members of his that are most closely united to him in glory. The *Inferno* begins with 'three blessed ladies' - the Mother of God, St Lucy, and Beatrice - coming to the rescue of the poet who has lost his way in the dark wood of worldliness. All that he sees thereafter is intended by God to lead him back to the path of holiness. The successor of St Peter, with his Christ-given authority, canonizes the saints with a similar purpose in mind. His burning ambition, the intention closest to his heart, is to help us to reach the celestial rose, to share the gladness and glory of the Queen of heaven and all the angels and saints in the immediate vision of the Most Holy Trinity. The teacher of all Christians wants his sons and daughters, as Dante did, to fear hell, to be ready for purgatory, and to walk humbly, on the path of faith, hope, and charity, towards paradise, the snow-white rose, the shining city of the saints, whose only lamp is the glorified lamb.

VI

SINCERE GIFT:
THE NEW FEMINISM OF
JOHN PAUL II

Léonie Caldecott

A few years ago, I was invited to an international conference on the role of women which was organized by the Pontifical Council for the Laity in Rome. Halfway through the conference we were told that we were to have an audience with the Holy Father. It was at a time when John Paul II's health was in a precarious state, before new and more effective drugs had helped to bring his condition at least partly under control. I listened with a mixture of awe and sympathy as he delivered, in a weakened voice, his address to us in French. But the real surprise was still to come. At the end of the address, he stood up and told Cardinal Stafford, who was hosting the conference, that he wished to greet each one of us individually.

There followed an extraordinary scene as hundreds of women, from all corners of the world, filed past Pope John Paul II. A number of women had brought with them albums

*This Chapter has been adapted from a contribution originally made to *Communio*, Spring 1993.

or writings, like children in a show-and-tell session. Through it all, the ailing pontiff remained on his feet, his head bowed in part by his illness, in part by the intimacy of each encounter, patiently smiling and blessing each and every one as she passed. As I got closer and closer to the Holy Father, I realized that some women were thanking him, as well as telling him things. I also noticed that instead of looking more and more tired, he was actually looking more alive, that even his voice seemed stronger and steadier. It was as if he were drawing strength from us, just as we drew encouragement from him. I was suddenly overwhelmed with the desire to be a part of that exchange. What can I give, poor as I am? What can I say, in just a few words... What can the heart contribute to the head?

*

In transforming culture so that it supports life, women occupy a place in thought and action which is unique and decisive. It depends on them to promote a 'new feminism' which rejects the temptation of imitating models of 'male domination,' in order to acknowledge and affirm the true genius of women in every aspect of the life of society, and overcome all discrimination, violence and exploitation. (99)

This is a passage from *Evangelium vitae* (1995), which sets out Pope John Paul II's prophetic vision of today's 'dramatic conflict between the "culture of death" and the "culture of life"'. An integral part of this vision is his call for a 'new feminism' - just as in earlier encyclicals he had called for a new evangelisation and a new theology of liberation. It is this new feminism which he envisages as the force which will enable women to resist the contemporary trend of regarding human life as just another factor to be eliminated or engineered to our own satisfaction.

As far as the right to life is concerned, every innocent human being is absolutely equal to all others. This equality is the basis of all authentic social relationships which, to be truly such, can be founded only on truth and justice, recognizing and protecting every man and woman as a person and not as an object to be used. (57)

The defence of life is, however, far from an isolated moral imperative. It is intimately connected with the *celebration* of life. We can 'reverence and honour every person' only if we rediscover a 'contemplative outlook' (83). It is an outlook that affects our attitude not only to human life, but to the entire cosmos - as the Pope has made clear on other occasions.[1] 'Such an outlook arises from faith in the God of life, who has created every individual as a 'wonder' (*cf. Ps* 139:14). It is the outlook of those who see life in its deeper meaning, who grasp its utter gratuitousness, its beauty and its invitation to freedom and responsibility. It is the outlook of those who do not presume to take possession of reality, but instead accept it as gift, discovering in all things the reflection of the Creator and seeing in every person his living image' (83).

This defence and celebration of life, this 'contemplative outlook,' the Pope sees as entrusted primarily to women. Here lies the great task and the starting point for a new feminism.

---

[1] For example, in his *Message for the World Day of Peace*, 'Peace with God the Creator: Peace with All of Creation' (1 January 1990).

Women for life?

The Pope's brief but weighty remarks on the role of women in the encyclical on life can be expanded with reference to the 1994 *Letter to Families*, the Message for the 1995 World Day of Peace ('Women: Teachers of Peace'), the *Letter to Priests* for Holy Thursday 1995, and the 1995 *Letter to Women*, together with the many talks and addresses given around the occasion of the UN's Beijing Conference. The main theological and exegetical work, of course, was accomplished in the apostolic letter *Mulieris dignitatem* (1988), on the 'Dignity and Vocation of Women on the Occasion of the Marian Year.' What the 1990s have brought is clearly a keener sense of the injustices to which women have been subjected throughout history, and which persist in large parts of the world. Many of the Pope's remarks in 1995 - and even aspects of the Holy See's official representations at the Beijing Conference itself - took the secular media by surprise.

Pope John Paul's respect and concern (indeed love) for women is evident in almost everything he writes, and many women respond to him with equal respect and affection. But 'old-style feminists' are not so happy. The Pope's respect for women may be genuine, but they suspect it is based merely on an intensely nostalgic love for his own mother, transferred to the Blessed Virgin and to an idealised image of femininity. Is 'motherhood' somehow intrinsic to being a woman, as the Pope always seems to imply? Is there such a thing as 'femininity'? Was the decision to restrict the priesthood to men in reality just a way of ensuring that women will never be allowed an influence in the running of the Church, despite all the rhetoric about equality?

Before showing how John Paul II is in fact responding to these questions, it is important to realise that there have always been many types of feminists, and many differences between them that no amount of 'sisterhood' could paper over. There are moderate feminists, and radical, separatist feminists. There are feminists who deny any intrinsic difference between men and woman (the extrinsic physical divergences being something that technology was expected eventually to overcome). But there are others, among whom are the 'eco-feminists', who believe in very radical differences, and believe that women - by virtue of their femininity, their closeness to nature, and other distinctive qualities - can in some way save the planet that is being subjected to the violent assault of a 'masculine' mentality.

However, the lack of concern even among eco-feminists for one particular kind of 'violent assault' on life, namely, that represented by abortion, represents an interesting lacuna. Amidst all the rhetoric about the insidious power of masculine technology, the long-term dangers of nuclear power and male indifference (or worse) to the female sphere of experience in the home or in personal relationships, there is within this movement a conspicuous silence about the significance of the central fact in most women's lives - the capacity to conceive and bear a child. The eco-feminists, in short, waver in front of the ideological stronghold of mainstream feminism on the issue of 'reproductive rights.' (It is important to note on the American scene the presence of 'pro-life feminists,' of whom Juli Loesch Wiley would be an outstanding example.[2])

---

[2] See, e.g., *Pro-Life Feminism*, ed. Gail Grenier Sweet (Toronto: Life-Cycle Books, 1985). Also, more recently, Naomi Wolf's cogent criticism of the internal inconsistencies in the moral reasoning and rhetoric of the pro-choice position.

Ironically, the same eco-feminists are often quite sympathetic to 'natural family planning,' purely on the grounds of respect for the nature of a woman's cycle.

John Paul II's statements on the significance and role of women in society coherently integrate all the moral and social questions that such women have been seeking, albeit selectively, to resolve. The synthesis is made possible thanks to the Pope's highly developed Christian anthropology. As an experienced pastor and friend to many, as a youth leader, and as a personalist philosopher from his days in Lublin, he has been uniquely equipped to locate the intrinsic value of every human life in the fact that it is the life of a *person* in the order of love and grace. Man and woman are fundamentally equal in that sense.

He further locates the meaning of human life in *love*, defined as the giving and receiving of the self. Marriage and parenthood, both human and divine, he sees as revealing love in its most intense and archetypal form. Thus he affirms the importance of a natural complementarity between men and women as such, intended by the Creator as the means by which the loving relations of the Trinity could be mirrored in the cosmos.

The nuptial mystery

John Paul II believes that God has revealed his own plan for human nature in revealing himself through Mary and Jesus, and that any Christian who reads the book of scripture and the book of nature with the eyes of faith - in the light of the Holy Spirit dwelling in the Church - will be able to discern there the features of man and woman as originally created and as presently redeemed. This is why he devoted so much time to expounding the book of Genesis in the Wednesday audiences at the beginning of his pontificate.

In his *Letter to Women*, the Pope also draws on Genesis (2:18-20). Reflecting on the complementarity of man and woman, he explains that woman is created by God to be a 'helper' for man not only in a physical or psychological sense - for the sake of reproduction or comfort - but *ontologically*, and for the task of transforming the earth through culture (*Letter to Women*, 7-8). Even in the task of salvation, this cooperation is evident: Mary complements Christ by the active receptivity of her *fiat*. By grace, she is raised (and in her the Church) to union with God in that love which is the eternal dance of the blessed Trinity.

In the Church, as Hans Urs Von Balthasar writes and the Pope echoes, the 'Marian' principle complements the 'Apostolic-Petrine' principle (11). But it is Mary, not Peter, who is supreme: as representative of humanity, she is 'Queen of the Apostles without any pretensions to apostolic powers: she has other and greater powers.'[3]

Given the Pope's 'nuptial' understanding of human nature as a 'unity of the two,' the first key to his new feminism must lie in the exegesis of the marriage covenant as one of *mutual subjection*, over against the simple subjection of wife to husband. There is still subjection, still obedience, still a distinction of roles, still complementarity, but it is a *mutual* subjection and therefore not 'oppressive.' This is how the Pope introduces the concept

---

[3] Balthasar's expression, quoted approvingly by the Pope in *Mulieris dignitatem*, fn. 55.

in *Mulieris dignitatem*, drawing out the implications of Ephesians 5:21:

> The text is addressed to the spouses as real women and men. It reminds them of the 'ethos' of spousal love which goes back to the divine institution of marriage from the 'beginning.' Corresponding to the truth of this institution is the exhortation: '*Husbands, love your wives*,' love them because of that special and unique bond whereby in marriage a man and a woman become 'one flesh' (*Gen* 2:24; *Eph* 5:31). In this love there is a fundamental *affirmation of the woman* as a person. This affirmation makes it possible for the female personality to develop fully and be enriched. This is precisely the way Christ acts as the bridegroom of the Church; he desires that she be 'in splendour, without spot or wrinkle' (*Eph* 5:27). One can say that this fully captures the whole 'style' of Christ in dealing with women. Husbands should make their own the elements of this style in regard to their wives; *analogously, all men should do the same in regard to women in every situation* [emphasis mine]. In this way both men and women bring about 'the sincere gift of self'.' (24).

Later on, the Pope concludes: 'In relation to the "old" this is evidently something "new": it is an innovation of the Gospel.' It is indeed new, a 'call which from that time onwards does not cease to challenge succeeding generations,' including our own. In its light we may locate the basis for this great Pope's call for a 'new feminism'.

Sincere gift

In a Lenten message[3a] to the Brazilian Church in 1990, John Paul II spelled out his vision for women in a particularly explicit way. Although the message is particularly aimed at a Latin culture (demonstrating the Pope's extraordinary sensitivity to the nuances, strengths and weaknesses of different civilisations), it nonetheless has universal reverberations.

> Woman ... is a person as much as man is; the person is the sole creature which God wanted for its own sake; the sole creature to be made expressly in the image and likeness of God, who is Love. Precisely for this reason, a person cannot find complete fulfillment except by making a sincere gift of self. Herein lies the origin of 'community,' in which the 'unity of the two' and personal dignity must be expressed, as much for man as for woman.

Woman, he goes on:

> ...finds her fulfilment and vocation as a person according to the richness of the attributes of femininity, which she received on the day of creation and which is transmitted from generation to generation, in her special manner of being the image of God, tarnished by sin and redeemed in Jesus Christ...
>
> The hardness of the human heart, wounded by the consequence of original sin in the passing of history, has harmed and upset the Creator's plan for woman... It is necessary for us now to walk down the paths of conversion, to return to the original vision of the Lord.

[3a] Reported in March/April 1990, *L'Osservatore Romano*.

Here and now I make my appeal to Brazilian woman and also appeal on her behalf: neither as slave, nor as queen, but just as woman:

- *Woman as child*: a person with the look of a simple but rare flower, blooming at the dawn of her life, she wants to receive and reflect God's light;

- *Woman in youth*: the sun of a spring morning, seen clearly, radiating hope, in need of respect, trust and dignity;

- *Adult woman*: the midday sun, with her simple dignity, sincerity and purity, giving light and warmth with serene reflection, with rectitude of spirit, with harmony, which is her wardrobe and adornment;

- *Elderly woman*: a welcoming shadow which falls with natural maternal affection and particular wisdom and prudence, living in self-gift, with the desire to serve the happiness of others, the happiness of her fellow creatures.

It is interesting to note that the first mention the Pope makes of the 'maternal' in this poetic tribute to the feminine genius in all its stages of development, is when he speaks of the older woman. He does not, as feminists might expect, automatically associate physical motherhood with the fertile years, but rather with an inner realisation of something which is the inheritance of every woman, and which is intimately bound up with what he calls the 'civilisation of love'. The special genius of women is concerned with the fact, not that all women are or should be mothers in the physical sense, but that womanhood is 'designed' with motherhood in mind, and therefore feminine strengths and sensibilities are orientated towards the welcoming and nurturing of life.

'A mother welcomes and carries in herself another human being, enabling it to grow outside her, giving it room, respecting its otherness' (*Evangelium vitae*, 99). While physical motherhood provides the template and key symbol for creating this culture of life, all women share a capacity to welcome the life of the other and to create the conditions for it to grow and flourish. Thus the true realization of the feminine genius is to be found in both home and public domain, in the office, the factory, the university or the convent; in political life, economic life, in the city or the country. There is not, therefore, a dichotomy among female vocations, say, to work or motherhood, to marriage or the cloister. They all issue from the same root: the capacity for spiritual motherhood.

John Paul II is supported in this vision by a long line of Catholic writers such as Edith Stein, Gertrude von le Fort, Caryll Houselander, and Adrienne von Speyr. For instance, on the primacy of men and women working alongside each other in the hierarchy of social interaction, the poet von le Fort wrote: 'Every sort of co-operation, even the most insignificant, between man and woman is, in its bearing upon the wholeness of life, of far greater import than associations that are purely masculine or purely feminine. Naturally, such associations have their definite purposes inasmuch as they are dedicated to a common struggle or ideal and serve for the development of certain new thoughts, but for limited scope only. In fact they risk sterility because of narrowness or one-sidedness and therefore are of little import in the wider cultural field.'[4]

---

[4] *The Eternal Woman* (Milwaukee: Bruce Publishing Co., 1962), 39.

Biology and beyond

John Paul II's most compelling exposition of the social, spiritual and eschatological significance of human motherhood can be found in *Mulieris dignitatem*. After taking a stand against the very biological reductionism falsely attributed to Catholic teaching by feminists,[5] he embarks on a profound exegesis of the maternal condition, an exegesis which illuminates all the essential points of Catholic moral teaching in this area, from the defence of life to the need for stable and faithful marriages. Rejecting any 'exclusively bio-physical interpretation of women and motherhood,' he links motherhood 'to the personal structure of the woman and to the personal dimension of the gift: 'I have brought a man into being with the help of the Lord' (*Gen* 4:1). And, whereas parenthood is something that belongs to both men and women, 'It is the woman who "pays" directly for this shared generation, which literally absorbs the energies of her body and soul. It is therefore necessary that *the man* be fully aware that in their shared parenthood he owes *a special debt to the woman*. No programme of "equal rights" between women and men is valid unless it takes this fact fully into account.' (Ref: 18) Men in some sense *learn their fatherhood from the mother of their children*, so that as the child grows, the contribution of both parents can come into play.

Mary's *fiat* signifies 'the woman's readiness for the gift of self and her readiness to accept a new life' (18). Through the perfection of her self-gift, made possible by the absence of original sin in her unclouded and lovely soul,

---

[5] See the satirization of this attitude in Margaret Atwood's *The Handmaid's Tale*.

the New Covenant is established: between God and man. Though imperfect in comparison, each fresh instance of motherhood in human history is nonetheless related to this central act on the part of Mary. The *'fiat* mentality' is the essential key to the fulfillment of a mother's vocation, not only at conception, but throughout the life of the child. This is the context for Jesus's response to the women in the Gospel of Luke: 'Blessed rather are those who hear the word of God and keep it' (11:27-28).

For John Paul II, this means that:

The motherhood of every woman, understood in the light of the gospel, is similarly not only "of flesh and blood": it expresses a profound *'listening to the word of the living God'* and a readiness to 'safeguard' this Word.... For it is precisely those born of earthly mothers, the sons and daughters of the human race, who receive from the Son of God the power to become 'children of God' *(Jn* 1:12). A dimension of the New Covenant in Christ's blood enters into human parenthood, making it a reality and a task for 'new creatures' *(cf. 2 Cor* 5:17). The history of every human being passes through the threshold of a woman's motherhood: crossing it conditions 'the revelation of the children of God' *(cf. Rom* 8:19). (19).

The entire passage about motherhood in *Mulieris Dignitatem* concludes with a meditation on Our Lord's use of the imagery of childbirth in John 16:21. 'The first part of Christ's words refers to the 'pangs of childbirth' which belong to the heritage of original sin; at the same time, these words indicate *the link that exists between the woman's motherhood and the Paschal Mystery.'*(19) There

is a hint here of the mysterious parallel between the
feminine vocation of motherhood and the masculine
vocation of the priesthood. In any case, the Pope goes on
to enumerate some of the sufferings which women go
through for the sake of this vocation, before focusing our
attention anew on the Resurrection. The key word here is
'joy' - 'the joy that a child is born into the world,' and
Jesus' words before his passion: 'I will see you again and
your hearts will rejoice, and no one will take your joy
from you' (*Jn* 16:22-23).

Elements of the new feminism

Mulieris dignitatem expounds all the essential elements
for the creation of the 'new feminism'. In addition to the
point about mutual subjection, there are four key
concepts to be noted:

1. The 'sincere gift of self,' of which the Blessed
    Virgin's *fiat* is the summit.
2. The 'debt' owed by men to women, who pay the
    heaviest price for the bearing of life.
3. The 'keeping of the Word' by women in their
    vocation, no matter what it is.
4. The conditioning of 'the revelation of the children
    of God' as the effect of the relationship between
    child and mother.

All four are inextricably linked, and necessary for the
process of cultural transformation envisaged by the
Holy Father.

Firstly, the acquiescence of women to what is asked
of them must be *sincere*, that is to say, arising out of a

deep conviction and sense of purpose. It must have a personal authenticity, the subject being defined in terms of her divine destiny, the will of God for her life, and not in terms of the *status quo*. Secular feminism has targeted the falsity of the feminine consciousness - for example the 1950s-style suburban housewife 'married to her house,' or the lack of integrity in the (Strindbergian) martyred or devouring mother. The woman of the sex-war, be she collaborator or guerilla, manifestly lacks both sincerity and the ability to give of her true self. This poor, 'unrepentant Eve' should hardly be mourned by anyone.[6]

Edith Stein too dwelled on this all-important principle of the 'sincere gift of self'. For her it is only in the profound communion with her Lord that a woman can find the strength to be truly herself.

The deepest longing of woman's heart is to give herself lovingly, to belong to another, and to possess this other being completely. This longing is revealed in her outlook, personal and all-embracing, which appears to us as specifically feminine. But this surrender becomes a perverted self-abandon and a form of slavery when it is given to another person and not to God; at the same time, it is an unjustified demand which no human being can fulfil. Only God can welcome a person's total surrender in such a way that one does not lose one's soul in the process but wins it. And only God can bestow himself upon a person so that He fulfils this

---

[6] It would require many pages of analysis to portray the permutations on this theme. Karl Stern's *The Flight from Woman* contains some interesting, if not definitive, material.

being completely and loses nothing of Himself in so doing. That is why total surrender, which is the principle of the religious life, is simultaneously the only adequate fulfilment possible for women's yearning.[7]

The second point gives us the absolutely necessary precondition *on the part of men* to the sincere gift of self on the part of women. If their surrender (whose true object is God) is met with ingratitude, or even a dishonourable and inappropriate complacency on the part of men, an offence is committed against both woman and her Creator, and disaster ensues. Misogyny is a very real phenomenon (even if it is exaggerated for the sake of the propaganda war between the sexes), and it is particularly crushing for a woman who presents herself with an attitude of good will and generosity. She may not resort to aborting the child in her womb (either literally or figuratively), but she can be so drained of strength by the encounter that she becomes incapable of effectively nurturing that which God has entrusted to her.

It is a curious paradox that women, when they are drained of strength (and hence tempted to despair), become ever more emphatic in their attempt to communicate. This desperation is apt to be interpreted as aggression, and thus the cycle of misunderstanding between the sexes is perpetuated. The Pope seems to be indicating that the key to ending this vicious cycle is in the hands of men. The sincere gift of self on the part of a woman can only be guaranteed and protected by a sincere rendering of the debt - a debt of gratitude and all the actions which ensue - on the part of our brothers in Christ.

---

[7] Edith Stein, *Woman*, trans. Freda Mary Oben (Washington: Institute of Carmelite Studies, 1987), 62.

So the third point concerns the necessity of long-term continuity in the woman's vocation, a continuity which has perforce to be rooted in the eternal. One of the Christian ideas which secular feminists object to is the emphasis on sacrifice. Yet there is no birth (or re-birth) without a certain blood-letting; there is no unconditional love without the preparedness to suffer. Is it worth speculating, however, on the distinction between the *preparedness* for sacrifice and the grim *determination* to carry it out? Could it be possible that there is a grain of truth in the secular crusade against an alleged Christian 'obsession' with suffering?

We are apt to slide into a kind of complacency with regard to Christ's passion and death which mirrors some men's complacency about female suffering. The redeemed Eve does not mind suffering torments to bring a child (or any other of God's works) into the world, and at her most sublime will accept that her labours not bear fruit until after her own death. Yet if God has called woman into being in order to *keep and protect* the Word, what shall we say of those who render this continuity through time difficult or even impossible? 'Troubles will come,' says the Lord, 'but woe to him through whom they come.' The Holy Father himself has exemplified this logic in his compassion for women who have wounded themselves through abortion.[8]

The image of abortion (literally 'putting out of its place') is an apt one. For woman can be said to have a womb-shaped vocation. She is a space-maker, a protector of

[8] See *Evangelium vitae* (99) where, interestingly enough, his thoughts pass immediately from the role of women in bringing about general cultural change, to the spiritual condition of women who have had abortions.

growth, an enabler of life, a place of safety where others can encounter Christ and know themselves to be loved. Hers is the mission to behold the world and all its confusing travail in a very particular way: to make use of her very weakness (*cf.* St Thérèse) to obtain the privileged place of the lamb which is carried upon the shoulders of the Shepherd, and thus see things from the perspective of His gaze. 'I love you as you are, for I see you as you are destined to be.' The eyes of a woman are thus a precious thing.

The final point is perhaps the most intriguing and profound ever made about the mystery of motherhood: 'The history of every human being passes through the threshold of a woman's motherhood: crossing it conditions "the revelation of the children of God."' (19) Here we see the weighty implications of Pope John Paul II's reflection on the maternal vocation. Nobody passes into the world without, as it were, passing through the 'ambience' of a woman. Woman has, even if only *in potentia*, an immense influence on the history of mankind. Her attitudes and outlook are paramount. So is her welfare, both physical and spiritual. The devaluing of motherhood, the degeneration of life-giving attitudes in the home and the assault on the concept of a love faithful unto death are all symptoms of a culture which has lost sight of that - (and we can be thankful that there are still cultures in the world today which maintain this awareness, as African and Asian women remind us).

It is, however, useless to point back to 'Victorian values' as the panacea: the problem goes much further back than that. As G.K. Chesterton put it, even in the Victorian household *the hearth was already cold*. Writing around the same period between the wars, Gertrud Von Le Fort echoed Chesterton's prophetic analysis. 'The feminist movement had its spiritual roots in the dullness and narrowness of the middle-class family. Its economic backgrounds do not concern us here. From the stress of their starving souls, the women of that period cried out for a spiritual purpose in life and for an activation of their capacity for love. It was a tragic motivation, for these women sought out a share of responsibility in the man's world, and sought it outside the family which could no longer shelter and satisfy them.'[9]

The new woman

In John Paul II's view, it is of course only through the covenant made in Christ Jesus - sealed in the heart of a real human woman, in one real moment of human history - that a cultural recovery is assured. It is the daughters of the Second Eve, whose transcendent humility called down the power of God upon earth - and those men who, like St Joseph, exercise unceasing and loving vigilance over their interests - who will turn the tide.[10]

The new woman is busy lowering her consciousness, not raising it, since it is humility (*humus* = earth or soil) which calls down the action of almighty God upon the earth. 'Be it done to me according to thy Word....' It is the Lord who does the raising, giving his own beauty in return for the sincere offering of her identity. The new feminist is truly a

---

[9] *The Eternal Woman*, 75.
[10] The theology of St Joseph and the meaning of fatherhood needs development, but for one prophetic attempt, see Andrew Doze, *Discovering St Joseph* (New York: Alba House, 1991).

daughter of the 'Mother of Fairest Love,' as the Holy Father dubbed Mary in his *Letter to Families*. She is truly free to do the will of the One who sent her, free to give without counting the cost. For she has inherited from her Mother the assurance of true motherhood, in which the economy of the virginal *fiat* is constantly renewed.

If justice is required, Mary is the Mirror of that justice, not the judge. If devotion is required, she is the Singular Vessel of that devotion, not herself the object of worship. Women can be tempted to turn themselves into goddesses, heroines of the hour in cosmic proportions. Whether she plays Gaia or Kali, it all amounts to the same: the sin of Eve, who listened to the serpentine words 'You shall be as gods.' 'Women for Life on Earth' is a beautiful ideal, but women are powerless to do more than wreak more havoc on earth, unless they are rooted in heaven. 'I will lift up mine eyes unto the hills, from whence cometh my help.' (*Ps* 121)

Through motherhood, whether physical or spiritual, John Paul II reminds us, women 'first learn and then teach others that human relations are authentic if they are open to accepting the other person: a person who is recognised and loved because of the dignity which comes from being a person and not from other considerations, such as usefulness, strength, intelligence, beauty or health. This is the fundamental contribution which the Church and humanity expect from women. And it is the indispensable prerequisite for an authentic cultural change'[11]

It is in this locus, at the heart of his social teaching and issuing out of the long tradition of mystical theology which

[11] *Evangelium vitae*, 99.

Pope John Paul II embodies, that his exegesis of the feminine condition must be understood. And since he gives the primacy of intuition to woman herself, I know he would not mind my ending these reflections by quoting a woman, Adrienne von Speyr:

> Every mother puts a surplus at her child's disposal, a kind of unlimited credit. Every mother has so much maternal love that even the most loving child cannot give it back to her - certainly not now, during the time of expectation. She keeps this surplus ready for the child, for his coming good and bad days. The Mother of the Lord also knows this secret. But over this, too, the grace of her Son has already disposed. So the Mother holds this surplus ready not only for her Child, out of her natural motherliness, but for all the plans, thoughts and concerns of the Child, not only in the measure of their worldwide extension, but also according to their divine, supernatural depths. The Mother's surplus of love in the expectation is already, even in concealment, flowing over onto the Church and the whole world.[12]

---

[12] Adrienne von Speyr, *Handmaid of the Lord* (San Francisco: Ignatius Press, 1985), 70.

VII

FACING THE SEXUAL REVOLUTION: JOHN PAUL II'S

LANGUAGE OF THE BODY

Agneta Sutton

From the beginning of his pontificate, Pope John Paul was faced (as his predecessor Paul VI had so tempestuously been) with the revolution in sexual mores within Western society and the development of modern birth control. He responded by exploring theologically the foundations of marriage and sexual love between man and woman. His response, that is, has not simply been a defence of the Church's existing teaching on marriage and procreation (and in particular of of Paul VI's Encyclical Letter *Humanae vitae*): he has also sought also to arrive at a more profound understanding of God's intentions in creating us man and woman and the meaning, in the eyes of God, of sexual love between man and woman united in marriage.

Many readers are familiar with John Paul II's Apostolic Exhortation *Familiaris consortio* of 1981 and with his *Letter to Families* of 1994 in which he speaks of the moral crises facing the modern world and the difficulties encountered by families trying to uphold traditional values.

Addressing himself to the world at large and in particular to Christian families, he speaks of the truth and love that should guide relationships between men and women and of the tensions and family breakdowns encountered by many because of darkened moral consciences. In both works he spells out the Catholic Church's teaching about sexual love and conjugal life. In both he speaks of spousal love as a cornerstone of civilisation and human society. Yet it is not in these two works that John Paul II explains in painstaking detail and at great length the theological basis and deep symbolism of marriage and of the sexual expression of conjugal love. For this we have to turn to his papal Wednesday lectures, delivered between 5 September 1979 and 28 November 1984.

This collection of lectures, published under the title *The Theology of the Body: Human Love in the Divine Plan*,[1] is a mystic's celebration of the human body and of human love.[2] Taking us on a spiritual journey in the light of the Gospel News, John Paul II makes not only a moral pronouncement to the effect that marriage should be a monogamous and indissoluble union, but he also tells us how we human creatures reflect God's love for us. We are told that our very embodiment as man or woman is symbolical and that our bodies speak a language. This is the language of the body revealed by Jesus Christ, who tells us that, by having created us men and women, different but complementary, God shows us that we are

---

[1] John Paul II, *The Theology of the Body: Human Love in the Divine Plan*, Pauline Books and Media, Boston, 1997.
[2] John Paul II is well versed in the mystic tradition, having written his first doctoral thesis on St John of the Cross.

relational beings, and that it is not so much singly as in union and communion, especially within marriage, that we resemble God and reflect his love for mankind.[3]

The language of the body

Given the windy roads John Paul II takes in the hundreds of lectures developing the language of the body, a summary of his itinerary at the outset of the journey will help the reader. True to his style, John Paul II's starting points for his arguments are Gospel passages. Turning first to the creation stories and Jesus' teaching that marriage should be a life-long faithful relationship, John Paul II explains that it was in their loving togetherness that man and woman were created in the image of God. They were created for love and their bodies were created for union and communion. In the beginning, before the Fall, their bodies were true instruments of union and communion. Then they, as embodied persons, spoke the language of the body as the language of creation. In particular, before sin entered on the stage man and woman, united in marriage founded on love, were the true image of God and a sign of God's love for us.

Having explored the language of creation, John Paul II spells out the language of the body with relation to fallen mankind. He tells us that Jesus reminds us that our bodies are made for union and communion and that true love and goodness comes from the heart. Truly good actions reflect

---

[3] John Paul II's understanding echoes that of Karl Barth who, in the volume on creation in his *Church Dogmatics* also spoke of the symbolism of our gendered nature and of man and woman as the image of God in their togetherness. Indeed, Hans Urs von Balthasar, commentator on Barth, and much admired by John Paul II, also speaks of the mystery of our bodily existence in his *Mysterium Paschale*.

an inner self that is good and loving. Thus Jesus calls man and woman united in marriage to express a love for one another in body and action that comes from the heart, a love that is full of respect for the other as a person. When the body speaks in this way as the voice of the heart, then it speaks the language of the body as the language of redemption, explains John Paul II.

Thirdly, developing the language of the body as the language of the resurrection, John Paul II tells us that in the resurrection our bodies will truly reflect the human heart; and the human heart will be at one with God. Body and soul will be truly one and the soul will be in harmony with God. In the resurrection, the body will reach perfection as an instrument of union and communion. Thus it will speak the language of the resurrection. However, in the resurrection, when the body reaches perfection it will serve as an instrument of union and communion in a virginal way. This is why the vocations of virginity and celibacy for the sake of the Kingdom of Heaven are special signs in the language of the resurrection, pointing to our future state in the world to come.

This in brief is the plot. What we have here is a three-stage divine drama - as a von Balthasar might say, or a Divine Comedy, in the words of a Dante.

The language of the body as the language of creation

That we are created as man and woman tells us about God's intentions. This very fact speaks to us as the language of creation and tells us that man and woman are meant for one another. In particular, it tells us that man and woman united in marriage built on love are created in the image of God and his ever faithful love for mankind. The language of creation can, however, only be truly understood with the help of Jesus Christ. It is he who decodes it. With reference to the Book of Genesis, he tells us that by creating us male and female God showed that he intended our bodies to serve as instruments for union and communion. he also tells us that from the beginning God intended marriage to be a special sign in the image of his own love for mankind.

Thus it is with reference to Jesus' dialogue with the Pharisees, related in Matthew 19 and Mark 10, that John Paul II develops the language of creation and begins the first act of his divine drama. In these Gospel passages we read that Moses' command about a writ of dismissal when a man divorces his wife was a human invention and that divorce was no part of God's intention in the beginning. To quote the Gospel of St Matthew, referring to Genesis 1:27 and Genesis 2:24, this is how Jesus answered the Pharisees who asked him about divorce:

> Have you not read that the Creator from the beginning made them male and female and that he said: This is why a man must leave father and mother, and cling to his wife, and the two become one flesh? They are no longer two, therefore, but one body. So then, what God has united, man must not divide (*Mt* 19:3-6).[4]

Jesus shows, then, that human beings are not meant to be alone but are called to interpersonal union and communion

[4] While John Paul II's understanding of the language of the body as the language of creation is spelled out mainly in *The Theology of the Body*, a synthesis of the argument is also found in John Paul II's Apostolic Letter, *Mulieris dignitatem* (On the Dignity of the Vocation of Woman).

and that lifelong faithful marriage is a special reflection of the Triune love and so of God's love for mankind.[5] That is, by creating us man and woman God told us that it is as relational beings we resemble Him Through Jesus we learn that when our bodies serve as instruments of union and communion, then we resemble God and as carnal creatures speak the language of the body as that of the creation. Thus John Paul II says: 'Man becomes the image of God not so much in the moment of solitude as in the moment of communion'.[6]

But the bliss of Paradise did not last long. It was soon spoilt by human sin. And sin blurred the language of creation. In the first story of creation in the Book of Genesis, we read that at the end of nearly every day of creation God observed his work and noted that it was good.[7] This tells us that the natural order, as God intended it, is good. But we have violated it and in so doing we have distorted the original order. Hence, we can no longer clearly see what God originally intended. This, says John Paul II, is why we fallen creatures have to turn to Jesus Christ in order to understand God's intentions for us.[8]

Three original experiences

So it is in the light of Jesus' references to the Book of Genesis in Matthew 19 and Mark 10, that John Paul II in his search for the original stamp placed on creation opens our eyes to three original experiences: *original solitude, original union* and *original innocence*. These are experiences

[5] *Theology of the Body*, 10 October 1979, pp.35-37. *Cf, Gen* 2:21.
[6] *Theology of the Body*, 14 November 1979, p.46.
[7] *The Theology of the Body*, 12 September 1979, p.29.
[8] *Theology of the Body*, 26 September 1979, pp.32-34.

belonging to man and woman as they were before the Fall. Yet, they also belong to man and woman as fallen, though now they are veiled by sin. They relate to human awareness of being special before God in virtue of our union-seeking nature, and the truth that it is in loving union and communion that we most realise our likeness to God.

Original solitude

It is Genesis 2:18-23 that gives expression to the experience of original solitude, explains John Paul II. Here we read that in God's view 'it is not good that man (male) should be alone', wherefore God made 'a helper fit for him'.[9] The passage reveals two kinds of experience of solitude: human awareness of being different from and superior to the animals; and human longing for a complementary companion and personal union and communion. One kind of solitude relates to our very nature as *Homo sapiens*, the other is 'derived from the male-female relationship'.[10]

The awareness of being superior to the animals was brought home to the human being when God asked Adam to name the animals (*Gen* 2:19). The awareness of being a relational being oriented towards love of another was revealed by Adam's joy at the sight of woman (*Gen* 2:23). The first realisation, then, relates to man's rationality and stewardship, whereas the second relates to man's longing for a helper fit for him, another being like himself, yet unlike himself and complementing him.[11] Indeed, referring

---

[9] *Theology of the Body*, 10 October 1979, p.36.
[10] *Theology of the Body*, 10 October 1979, p.35.
[11] *Theology of the Body*, 10 October 1979, pp.35-37.

to our union-seeking nature in the image of God, the second realisation also reflects the truth that we are oriented towards union with God.

The second realisation, then, points to two kinds of personal union and communion, namely the spousal one and union and communion with God. Thus, implicit in the concept of original solitude is the understanding that man, as the only creature created for personal union and communion, is the only creature created in the image of God and chosen by God to be his covenant partner.[12] And so man is the only creature of whom God demands self-conscious love and obedience. For among all the earthly creatures, humans alone are capable of apprehending the otherness, might, love and command of God and of choosing to follow or to turn away from him.[13]

In short the concept of original solitude tells us about our unique relationship with God and our longing for love as relational beings in the image of God.

Original union

The concept of original union is also revealed in Genesis 2:18-23, where we read that Adam was put to sleep by God only to wake up to find to his joy a helper truly fit for him.[14] It is Adam's exclamation of joy that tells us that in woman he recognises a person with whom he may communicate and share his life.[15] His joy confirms that in woman, in her difference and complementary to himself,

[12] *Theology of the Body*, 24 October 1979, p. 38; 14 November 1979, pp.45-48.
[13] *Theology of the Body*, 10 October -14 November, pp.35-48.
[14] *Theology of the Body*, 7 November 1979, pp.43-45.
[15] *Theology of the Body*, 9 January 1980, pp.63-66.

he sees a true life-companion. It is the joy found in the recognition that we are meant for love and that there is someone to love and to be loved by. It is the joy found in the recognition of the beauty of man-woman love, especially exclusive and faithful man-woman love realised in marriage. It is the joy and wonder of man-woman love as God intended it in the beginning, in the likeness of his love for mankind, says John Paul II.

The concept of original union tells us, then, about the beauty of human love, in the image of God's love for us.

Original innocence

That man and woman, in their original union, were alienated neither from one another nor from God is revealed in Genesis 2:23-25.[16] In the beginning, they were in their union and communion, a true reflection of the One and Triune God. The mutual self-gift of man and woman stained by no sin, was disturbed by no selfish and unruly passions.[17] The human person experienced no disunion between his desires and what he knew was right and good. Before the Fall, human desires and aspirations were in perfect harmony with the human will, which was in harmony with the will of God.

The concept of original innocence tells us about the harmony that reigned between God and mankind and within the realm of human relationship before sin entered the stage. But ever since the Fall, humanity experiences unruly passions, loss of self-control and a blurred

[16] *Theology of the Body*, 2 January 1980, pp.57-60.
[17] *Theology of the Body*, 30 January 1980, p.68.

perception of right and wrong, notes John Paul II. This leads to selfish actions that are disrespectful of other people. It leads to disunion in human relations. This is true not least in man-woman relationships. And this is why the Fall blurs the meaning of the language of the body, the language about the symbolism of our being created male, and of the female, which points to our union-seeking nature and our true image.[18]

In the state of original innocence, when the human body spoke the language of creation, the body was truly an instrument of union and communion. But this is no longer so. After the Fall the human body became partly an instrument of alienation and the human being's likeness to God was blurred.[19] Concupiscence, greed and pride took hold of the human being and obscured the language of the body. Thus the body is no longer a true instrument of union and communion.

The language of the body as the language of redemption

The language of redemption relating to man's fallen state speaks of the restoration of fallen humankind through Jesus Christ and through the grace of the Spirit. John Paul II's development of the language of redemption is much in the spirit of St Thomas's reflections on 'the Law of the Gospel' in the *Summa Theologiae*, where we read that the New Law proclaimed by Christ is first and foremost, and an inward one. For 'it is the grace of the Holy Spirit, given through faith in Christ, that is predominant in the law of the New

---

[18] *Theology of the Body*, 16 January 1979, pp.63-66.
[19] *Theology of the Body*, 30 April 1980, pp.108-111.

Covenant'.[20] Hence, act two of John Paul II's divine drama presenting the language of redemption should also be understood as presenting an argument against Pelagianism, that is, against the view that man can be saved by his own efforts alone. For John Paul II says that Jesus reinterpreted the language of creation blurred by sin and told us that restoration of the order of creation begins with the restoration of the heart of man through faith and grace.

Thus, with reference to Matthew 5:27-28, John Paul II explains that mere outward behaviour and obedience to the laws of God are not enough to reflect God's will. Our actions must reflect an inner self of love for God and neighbour, inspired by grace and faith in Jesus Christ. Only then do we as bodily creatures speak the language of the body as the language of redemption.[21]

The language of redemption, then, is a language of body and heart, entailing love of God and neighbour. It entails a respectful attitude towards others, not least towards members of the opposite sex. It entails self-giving and selfless love between man and woman in marriage. In his Sermon on the Mount, Jesus said: 'You have heard that it was said, "You shall not commit adultery". But I say to you that everyone who looks at a woman lustfully has already committed adultery with her in his heart' (*Mt* 5:27-28). These words represent Christ's fundamental revision of the moral law of the Old Covenant, of the Old Testament understanding of

---

[20] Thomas Aquinas, *Summa Theolgiae*, 1a 2ae, q106.
[21] Much of John Paul II's argument against Pelaginasim is presented in his lectures on St Paul's teaching on the body. I have not dealt with them here, as I have rested only at the major stops on John Paul II's road mapping out the language of the body.

the law.[22] These are the words that shift the emphasis from mere external obedience to man's attitude to God and neighbour. They are a call to make the body the mouthpiece of a pure heart and thus a true vehicle of union and communion.

But the meaning of the human body as an instrument for union and communion is obscured by selfish desires as is especially obvious 'in the sexual order'.[23] 'Concupiscence in itself drives man towards possession of the other as an object'.[24] It depersonalises the other person and reduce him or her to an object of gratification.[25] Jesus' words concerning adultery in the heart show us that for a man to look lustfully at a woman, seeing her as an object for pleasure or use, is to devalue her. Thus, as John Paul II observes, adultery in the heart can be committed even within marriage. This is because 'adultery in the heart is committed not only because man looks in this way at a woman who is not his wife, but precisely because he looks at a woman in this way'.[26] By 'this way' is meant a way that reduces woman to a mere object and fails to respect her as a person.

While the Old Testament ethics tended to be legalistic, what Jesus calls for is a new attitude. In particular, he calls for love and respect between man and woman. His emphasis is on the interior dimension of obedience to God.[27] 'To reach it, it is not enough to stop at the surface of human actions. It is necessary to penetrate inside' (*ibid.*).

---

[22] *Theology of the Body*, 16 April 1980, p.103.
[23] *Theology of the Body*, 28 May 1980, p.115.
[24] *Theology of the Body*, 30 July 1980, p.130.
[25] *Theology of the Body*, 30 July 1980, p.128.
[26] *Theology of the Body*, 8 October 1980, p.157.
[27] *Theology of the Body*, 16 April, 1980, p.105.

Jesus' appeal to the human heart calls fallen man to overcome his alienation from God and neighbour and all the distortions in man-woman relationships due to disordered desires. It is, a 'demand, so to speak, that man should re-enter into his full image'.[28] It is a call to make the body an instrument of the Gospel ethos and so speak the language of redemption.

The language of the body as the language of the resurrection

Having staged the created order as it was in the beginning and having told us about our role in the second act of his divine play, John Paul II opens the curtains to present the third act about the Kingdom of Heaven to come. His argument begins with an analysis of Jesus' discussion with the Sadducees, 'who "say that there is no resurrection"' (*Mt* 22:23). It then returns to Jesus conversation with the Pharisees about marriage and divorce. While we are told that marriage is a sign not only in the order of creation but also a sign anticipating the world to come, it is explained that virginity or celibacy for the sake of the Kingdom of Heaven anticipates, even more clearly than the monogamous and indissoluble Christian marriage, our ultimate union and communion with God when our bodies, as perfect instruments of union and communion, will speak the language of the resurrection.

The Sadducees 'treated the question of resurrection as a hypothesis which might be disproved'.[29] For this Jesus

---

[28] *Theology of the Body*, 23 April 1980, p.107.
[29] *Theology of the Body*, 18 November 1981, p.236.

rebuked them,[30] observes John Paul II, chastising the sceptics who question the literal veracity of the resurrection stories. Affirming the truth that Jesus rose from the dead and the reality of the Kingdom Heaven to come, he even tells us that we are bringing that future Kingdom closer by following Jesus' call to our hearts, and thus with the help of the Spirit, start building the Kingdom of Heaven.

Concluding his dialogue with the Sadducees about the resurrection, Jesus says that when God spoke to Moses he called himself 'the God of Abraham, the God of Isaac and the God of Jacob' (*Mt* 22:32). He tells the Sadducees that God is the God of the living, the God of the resurrection.[31] Jesus even tells the Sadducees something about life in the resurrection. He says: 'When they rise from the dead, they neither marry nor are given in marriage' (*Mk* 12:25), indicating that in the resurrected state man reaches a new perfection.[32] For in the resurrection we will be closely united with God. Marriage here on earth is a good thing willed by God. Yet it is but a reflection of God's loving plan and a more perfect union to come in the Kingdom of Heaven. Thus Jesus tells the Sadducees that in Heaven we shall reach a new perfection different from that before the Fall and that marriage will be no part of man's heavenly future because in heaven it is not needed, explains John Paul II. That is, he shows that marriage is a sign in this world of God's love and his divine plan and that procreation as a good of marriage also belongs to this world only.

---

[30] *Cf. Mt* 22:24-30; *Mk* 12:18-27; *Lk* 20:27-40.
[31] *Theology of the Body*, 18 November 1981, p.236.
[32] *Theology of the Body*, 2 December 1981, p.238.

While sin has blurred our likeness to God, and while attention to Jesus' appeal to our hearts restores and redeems, in the resurrected state we will, more perfectly than ever on earth, embody the image of God. By saying of those who have been resurrected that 'they are equal to angels and sons of God, being sons of the resurrection' (*Lk* 20:30), Jesus tells us that in the resurrected state not only will the soul be fully at one with the body in the sense that we will no longer be subject to disordered desires, but our hearts will be fully at one with God. Harmony will reign between man and God, and so between human beings and between body and soul. As the fruit of grace, we will be 'spiritualised', that is, 'the spirit will dominate the body'.[33] And ruled by a spirit united with God, the body will speak the language of the body as that of the resurrection, says John Paul II.

In short, in the resurrection, we will rediscover the true meaning of the body as a vehicle for union and communion. But this will be in a virginal way. And yet, as carnal beings we will retain our sexual differences.[34] We will not lose our psychosomatic identities. But, since the carnal love expressed in marriage and required for procreation is no part of humankind's future in heaven, the human being will respond to 'the gift of Himself on God's part', by a virginal love.[35] Hence, it is in a new non-sexual self-giving that the human being will truly discover himself as a relational being, a being made for union and communion with God, a being fully in the image of God of love.

---

[33] *Theology of the Body*, 9 December 1981, p.241.
[34] *Theology of the Body*, 13 January 1982, pp.243-244.
[35] *Theology of the Body*, 16 December 1981, p.244.

Celibacy and virginity for the sake
of the Kingdom of Heaven

It is precisely because our union and communion with God in heaven will be of the virginal kind that virginity and celibacy for the sake of the Kingdom of Heaven reflect even more clearly than the monogamous and indissoluble marriage our future state in the resurrection. This, says John Paul II, is what Jesus explained when talking to the Pharisees about marriage, widowhood and celibacy. Replying to the disciples who said about that the requirement that marriage should be an indissoluble union that it is a hard one, Jesus said: 'Not all men can receive the precept, but only those to whom it is given. For there are eunuchs who have been so from birth, and there are eunuchs who have been made eunuchs by men, and there are eunuchs who have made themselves eunuchs for the sake of the Kingdom of Heaven. He who is able to receive this, let him receive it' (*Mt* 19:11-12).

By this reply, which 'did not directly take a position in regard to what the disciples said', Jesus pointed to the significance of marriage as a sign in the language of the body as the language of creation, while at the same time declaring that the renunciation of marriage for the sake of the Kingdom of Heaven is the primary sign of God's future plan for mankind.[36] In other words, Jesus told the disciples that the vocations of virginity and celibacy for the sake of the Kingdom of Heaven are special signs in the language

---

[36] *Theology of the Body*, 10 March, 1982, p.263. John Paul II position represents a firm stand against those who say that *Mt* 19:11-12 is not to be interpreted as being about celibacy as well as against Protestant theologians, like Karl Barth, who dismiss the vocations of celibacy and virginity for the sake of the Kingdom of Heaven.

of the resurrection, special signs pointing to our virginal union with God in Heaven. He also told them that these vocations require a special grace and that, therefore, nobody is commanded to adopt this way of living. The special grace is that of the gift of being able to make a sacrifice, which actually emphasises the value of marriage. What Jesus is saying is that virginity for the sake of the Kingdom of Heaven is a 'donation of self to God in virginity', which anticipates man's future resurrection and union with God in a way that complements the symbolism of marriage and shows us more clearly what God has in mind for us in the world to come.

No doubt the Pharisees and the disciples were amazed by the words of Jesus. Being brought up in the Old Testament tradition, it would have been difficult for them to understand the significance of virginity and celibacy for the sake of the Kingdom of Heaven. Virginity and celibacy for the sake of the Kingdom of Heaven have no place in the Old Testament where fertility is praised in anticipation of the birth of the Messiah of Israel.[37] Pointing not to the coming of a reign of this world but to that of the next, virginity and celibacy for the sake of the Kingdom of Heaven are signs not of earthly, but of spiritual, fruitfulness, 'a fruitfulness different from that of the flesh', a 'supernatural fruitfulness of the human spirit which comes from the Holy Spirit'.[38]

John Paul II's interpretation entails, however, no denigration of the vocation of marriage. He emphasises that both marriage and the vocations of virginity and celibacy

---

[37] *Theology of the Body*, 17 March 1982, pp.264-267.
[38] *Theology of the Body*, 24 March 1982, pp.268-269.

for the sake of the Kingdom of Heaven are, in their different ways, instruments of grace that help to turn the body into a vehicle for union and communion. His point is that the vocations of virginity and celibacy for the sake of the Kingdom of Heaven point more explicitly than that of marriage to our future state in the resurrection. His main concern, however, is marriage and so his divine play ends with reflections on St Paul's Letter to the Ephesians and the Song of Songs, both of which are eulogies of the charism of marriage and of the body as an instrument of love.

The Letter to the Ephesians and the Song of Songs

The Letter to the Ephesians, which develops the analogy between spousal love and Christ's love for the Church, shows that the Church itself is the 'great sacrament, that is, the great visible sign and manifestation of the New Covenant'.[39] Comparing the two signs, the Church and marriage, St Paul is thinking of husband and wife as an organic unity. The Ephesian analogy speaks of Christ as the head and of the Church as the body and, thus by analogy, refers to the husband as the head and the wife as the body within the spousal union. But this analogy should not be taken to imply male superiority, says John Paul II. It does not represent a call for one-sided respect for the husband on the part of the wife.[40] That the husband is described as the head and the wife as the body means that their union is organic in the sense that it is only in their togetherness that they constitute a whole in the image of Christ's union with the Church. The analogy

[39] *Theology of the Body*, 27 October 1982, p.342.
[40] *Theology of the Body*, 11 August 1982, pp.309-311.

points to the intimacy of the union of Christ and Church and, therewith, shows that it is not so much singly as in intimate union and communion in marriage that man and woman reflect Christ's union with the Church-and therewith bear witness to his appeal to the human heart and so start building the Kingdom of Heaven here on earth.

By describing the Church as the body of Christ, the analogy ascribes a special dignity to the human body as an instrument of the Spirit, as an instrument of union and communion. 'The comparison with the Church as the Body of Christ, the body of his redemptive and at the same time spousal love, should leave in the minds of those to whom the letter of the Ephesians is destined a profound sense of the "sacredness" of the human body'.[41]

While the Ephesian letter is one of praise for the body, nowhere in the Scriptures is the body and bodily love more celebrated than in the Song of Songs, which speaks of the very sexual act within marriage as unifying and symbolising God's love for mankind. 'The Song of Songs is invested with all the richness of the language of human love', exclaims John Paul II.[41a] Speaking of the body as a vehicle of union and communion, the book speaks of a love that is respectful of the other as a person as an equal in the image of God, as is made clear when the groom calls his beloved, his sister. The word 'sister' speaks of kinship and a 'reciprocal and disinterested gift'.[42] It points to a relationship of two people sharing the same origin, that of being children of God. It points to a relationship of solidarity, of feeling at one.

[41] *Theology of the Body*, 1 September 1982, p. 321.
[41a] *Theology of the Body*, 23 May 1984, pp. 368-369.
[42] *Theology of the Body*, 30 May, 1984, p.371.

Thus John Paul II closes his three-stage divine drama by celebrating sexual love itself inasmuch as it an expression of spiritual union and so of committed, exclusive and faithful spousal love. As an expression of love, sexual union itself is shown to be a reflection of divine love, an expression through which the body realises its true potential as a vehicle of union and communion.

Conclusion

John Paul II's language of the body as the languages of creation, redemption and the resurrection is the language of the human body as male and female and of the meeting- as well as virginal or celibate non-meeting - of two sexually different human beings. He shows that as embodied and sexually differentiated beings we are acting out a divine drama. Taking us on a spiritual journey, he shows that our bodies are meant as vehicles for union and communion. Thus, leading us through the Scriptures with focus on the Gospels he tells us that, while the relationship with God of those who devote their lives to him in virginity or celibacy is a more transparent sign of our future union with God in heaven, no human relationship better reflects divine love than that founded on love between husband and wife.˙

˙I am much indebted to Professor Michael Banner under whose sympathetic and encouraging supervision I wrote my Doctoral thesis on John Paul II's sexual ethics.

VIII

THE SOCIAL TEACHING OF JOHN PAUL II AND ITS IMPLICATIONS FOR CATHOLIC EDUCATION FOR LIFE

Rodger Charles SJ

JOHN PAUL II BRINGS CATHOLIC SOCIAL TEACHING TO ITS MATURITY

Background: Karol Wojtyla's experience of the degradation of man

The modern social teaching of the Church developed from *Rerum novarum* of Leo XIII (1891) - though there were social encyclicals before that and the social teaching tradition goes back to the scriptures. That John Paul II should be Pope at the end of the disastrous 20th century, when that social teaching became so important, was singularly a blessing to the Church and the world. Living under the Nazis from 1939, he, like all Poles went in fear of his life and he worked as a quarryman for four years in order to escape their clutches while studying clandestinely. Then, from 1945 under the Communists, he had to face a more subtle but no less real persecution of a people. Such experience made him determined to proclaim above all the human dignity which he had seen so violated under these totalitarianisms. *Redemptor hominis*, 'The redeemer of man' (1979), his first encyclical (and first encyclicals tend to contain the essence of a particular Pope's agenda), deals with the theological foundations of human dignity. Christ is the perfect man, who restored in the children of Adam the likeness of God. 'By his incarnation, he, the Son of God, has in a certain way, united himself with each man. He worked with human hands, he thought with a human mind, acted with a human will and with a human heart he loved' (8).

All, then, should be treated justly as brothers and sisters of Christ. As a young man he was early interested in problems of social justice, and the social teaching of the Church as a way of building a new and better Poland. Gifted as actor, writer, poet, linguist and dramatist, his intention was to make a career in the arts. He was always, also, an action man enjoying soccer, skiing, canoeing, and mountaineering.

When, in 1941 war circumstances turned his mind to the priesthood, gifts as a theologian and philosopher meant doctoral and postdoctoral studies in these subjects. As a priest he did a great deal of pastoral work, which he loved; rich and poor, men and women, young and old, educated and not educated, all found in him a friend, always. He was active as writer, playwright and poet and had the widest range of friends in the arts, the sciences, and the professions. Professor of social ethics at Lublin in 1956, he was Bishop in 1958, Archbishop in 1964, and Cardinal in 1969. A key figure in the Second Vatican

Council, he greatly influenced *Gaudium et spes* and *Dignitatis humanae*, the two documents concerned with justice in society and human rights.

Liberation theology and human rights

As Pope, one of the first tasks he had to face was the burgeoning of liberation theology, in Latin America especially. At the Latin American Bishops Council (CELAM) at Puebla, Mexico, in January 1979, it was a central issue. A valid and necessary concept in itself, some naively thought liberation could be combined with baptizing Marx and adopting his social analysis. John Paul was not impressed. He had pondered, and rejected, the use of violence in search of social justice, as a young dramatist working on the life of St. Albert - a 19th century Pole who worked with the poor; while his close acquaintance with real socialism revealed it for the disaster it was. On January 19th he told the Mexican priests and religious they were not political leaders but men of God, centres of unity in the Church. Addressing the Bishops on the 20th, he stressed that the truth about Christ does not warrant any interpretation of his life as that of the social revolutionary from Nazareth.

The truth about the Church is that her mission is to proclaim, to all, the kingdom of Christ, not just to one social class. The truth about man is that the primordial anthropology of Genesis does not accommodate the idea of him as a mere fragment of nature, for he is made in God's image. On the 21st he addressed half a million Indians in Cuilapan announcing himself as the champion of those poor who knew much of deprivation.

That he had himself had experience of backbreaking labour that did not render the necessities of a truly decent life, made his heart go out to them and their loved ones. Justice must be done, the necessary reforms must be put in place. Then, in Poland in June 1979, he began that process of encouraging his fellow countrymen to insist on recognition of their human dignity and their right to freedom, and to do so peacefully, which miraculously would ten years later enable them to claim it.

He has issued three strictly social encyclicals, but the message of human rights and social justice has been at the heart of all his pastoral visits across the world while many of his other encyclicals and official documents touch on the same. To *Redemptor hominis* we have already referred. *Dives in misericordia* shows the need for love as well as justice in dealing with social problems; the Apostolic Constitution *Familiaris consortio* (1981) and the Apostolic Letter *Mulieris dignitatem* (1998) deal with the family, which is the basis of state and church, and with the dignity of women respectively, while *Veritatis splendor* and *Evangelium vitae* show how basic are sound moral values to a just society.

Laborem exercens: the dignity of human work

Man as worker is the theme of the encyclical *Laborem exercens*. It is the most comprehensive and coherent in-depth treatment given to any one particular aspect of the Church's social teaching. His own experience of hard manual work taught him to reflect deeply on these things in the light of the scriptures. The encyclical starts by reminding us that man is placed in the world by God to work it and so earn his daily bread: this is a mark of his role as a person. The Church took up the cause of the workers in *Rerum novarum* (1891) and this new encyclical document is one with it (1-3). In working, man imitates his creator (4) and in God's plan work is always personal, subjective, done by one who is a person, conscious of that. Work is objective(5), its end product is important and as such it is valued in different ways, but whatever honest work a man does, however humble, gives him human dignity which demands respect. We do not value people by what they do. We value them and their work by what they are, sons and daughters of God (6). The liberal capitalist in the 19th century did not do this (7) and the workers reaction in solidarity was justified (8). Work is sometimes hard, this is the penalty that sin placed on man and the Christian will join his suffering in this to those of his master, Christ. Industriousness, meanwhile, is a moral habit which makes man good (9).

Liberal capitalism produced the Marxist reaction and the theory of social revolution leading to communism, so opposing capital and labour (11). But while the Church teaches that labour has priority over capital, capital and labour cannot be opposed (13): the production process emphasises this. The only legitimate title to the possession of goods, private or public, however, is their service of labour. Proposals for enabling wage earners to share in management, ownership or profits are therefore significant in this context (14).

The more personal approach to the relationship between capital and labour, and the rights and obligations of labour are then considered (15). Direct and indirect employers must do their part in providing the conditions in which these can be secured. The worker has a right and a duty to work (17-18), to adequate wages and conditions (19), to organise in trade unions working for justice constructively, in a spirit of solidarity, not class egoism (20).

Sollicitudo rei socialis (1987): social justice world-wide

This encyclical deals with the way in which the universal purpose of created things is achieved by economic justice between nations (5-10). When Paul VI published his *Populorum progressio* in 1977, there was more optimism about overcoming the problems of world poverty in all its aspects (12). The blame for later pessimism rests on rich and poor nations alike. The rich for operating economic, financial and social mechanisms which often penalise the poorer, while the èlites in less developed countries have too often failed in doing what they could and should do, to help their country's self-development (16). Problems are caused by the conflicts between the power blocs and by the failure to come to terms with demographic changes (19 -25). There are, however, positive signs, for example the growing awareness of human rights, of the respect for life itself in the face of abortion or euthanasia, the concern for the environment and for peace and justice (26).

There are moral problems of development. In itself, it is a good and a necessary process. But it should not mean over-development, which harms the environment, moral as well as physical, while leading to consumerism (27-30). We should not despair of solving these problems, but with faith in God, and with co-operation between peoples and respect for human rights, solidarity and respect for our world, we should seek answers (31-34). In fact there has been and is selfishness, lack of vision and moral principle; it is right to speak of structures of sin caused by excessive concentration on profit and power. Conversion of heart alone is the answer to these; it leads to true solidarity; those with economic power should use that power justly, while those without it should do what they can for the common good, being neither passive nor threatening to destroy the social fabric (35-38). Peace is the work of justice and, by extension, of solidarity. The Church tries to give moral guidance. It is not in her remit to recommend or enact specific political or economic solutions or systems. She will condemn the evils she sees; but more positively she will try to support policies that are aimed at real and just solutions (41- 45). A liberation theology which respects the values set out in the documents of the social magisterium (e.g. *Libertatis conscientia*), will help in this. Solidarity is above all solidarity with the poor (46-49).

Centesimus annus: social perfection and the common good

The attempt to build perfect social systems dehumanises man. A humane society must harmonise self-interest with the common good. Hitler's Nazi paradise, the evil Thousand Year Reich lasted 12 years, Stalin's Soviet equivalent more than 40. The collapse of the latter began in 1989, just before the one hundredth anniversary of *Rerum novarum. Centesimus annus*, 'On the hundredth anniversary', celebrated that document which guided a Catholic Church in Europe and the USA which was confused about how to respond to liberal capitalism. John Paul condemned its excesses. He also condemned the

Communist idea of the social ownership of productive goods. Only economic freedom will provide the wealth with which their needs will be met. He was remarkably prescient. It was the inability of the Marxist command economy to meet the needs of the people that lay behind its rejection by the people, but until the 1970s that seemed a long way away.

In the meantime, since 1917, the world had been racked by tensions between the two systems; many Westerners perversely thought the Communist system best, though they carefully avoided living under it. When in the 1980s it became apparent that the monolith was imploding, the only question was, would it do so peacefully or in violence? It is here that John Paul's experience, wisdom and knowledge, put the world for ever in his debt because it was the lead he gave to his fellow countrymen in reclaiming civil society peacefully, by insisting on human rights and responsibilities, that finally by 1989 had sapped the strength of Polish Communism and so gave the example to others that it could all be done with minimal violence.

Some said that the collapse of the Soviet system marked the end of history. It did not, of course; but it was the end of the debate on what was the best social system: it is one in which personal, social, political and economic freedom exist. Sadly, Western freedom, in fact, is severely defective, as *Centesimus annus* points out.

It takes *Rerum novarum* as the starting point (1-10). That document centred on the dignity of man and the state's duty to the common good in responsible freedom (11). Today, there is still need in some circumstances to face conflict in the search for justice, but not the Marxist way (14). The world rejected the totalitarian Communist system after 1989, peaceful Poland showing the way (22-24). We must look to the future *not* looking for a perfect social system; self-interest must be harmonised with the common good, otherwise bureaucracy stifles freedom (25). The earth was given to all and all must share its wealth. This is done primarily by work and that means know-how, technology and skill, foreseeing the needs of others, and supplying those needs at a just price in a free, morally responsible market (30-31). All should have access to the market though many, through poverty, do not; individuals and countries must be given that access by those who are fortunate to have it themselves (33-34). If this is done, the free market is most efficient in the use of resources (33). Profit is a good if it is a measure of that efficiency, achieved with human and moral needs respected (35).

In the third world especially, conditions are often as bad as in the nineteenth century and unions must seek for justice, not for socialism which has failed, but 'a society of free work, enterprise and participation which meets the needs of the whole society'. Capitalism as we know it is not the only alternative (35). That capitalism produces consumerism. It does not distinguish between needs which foster, and needs which undermine, the human person so that evils such as drugs are seen as goods. It is not wrong to live better; it is wrong to make goods an end in themselves (36). Consumerism ravages the physical and moral environment, marriage and family especially (37-9). Economic life has become absolutised; the market becomes the subject of idolatry. Economic freedom is only one aspect of freedom which must primarily be spiritual and religious (40).

Western society is alienated as its work system and its members use one another in the pursuit of wealth and mass communications manipulate them (41). Is capitalism then, the model for the world? It is better to say that the market economy, private ownership of productive goods, business creativity in a strong juridical framework at the service of human freedom (the core of which is ethical and religious) is the model (41). In fact the danger now is of a radical ideology, of freedom that knows no restraint (42). What we should be seeing is an ownership of the means of production that serves useful work; that is their purpose (43).

The political system must be based on freedom, but modern democracy, which rejects the idea of ultimate truth, leads to totalitarianism; absolute values which safeguard human rights alone protect true freedom (44-46). In pursuit of the common good the state should foster the conditions which produce a sound market system. It can intervene to prevent poverty and deprivation by helping people to get out of them; but a social assistance state is self-defeating. Voluntary services, however, foster self-help (48). The Church has a role in helping to create solidarity and charity (49-52). Her message enriches human dignity (55); it stresses the preferential option for the poor. The solution to national problems lies in the co-operation which liberal capitalism and Marxism rejected (60). The world is more aware today of the need for religious values in reform and the Church knows that Almighty God has given his Church to lead man into the third millennium, along with Christ her Lord and Mary his mother in a pilgrimage of faith (62). John Paul II has brought the Church's social teaching to its maturity. That his life experience has included the struggle with poverty and his opposition to Nazism and Communism gives him sound credentials, and his wide and profound learning confirms them.

THE MATURATION OF CATHOLIC SOCIAL TEACHING

John Paul II has, in the first place, woven the foundation principle of Catholic social teaching, that man, redeemed by Christ is the purpose and end of every social organization, so firmly into the social teaching of the Church that it has given it a new and a needed coherence. At Puebla he rejected the illusions of a Christian Marxism because of what it had done to man, while insisting that the deep set problems of poverty cry to heaven and must be addressed because they affront human dignity. In *Laborem exercens* he showed the dignity of work and worker which liberal capitalism with its worship of profit, Nazism with its slave camps and Stalin's Gulags denied, and which capitalism today has not fully accepted. *Sollicitudo rei socialis* emphasised the failure of the richer nations to do their part fully to see to all mankind having access to the means to gain an adequate livelihood; and of the èlites in the poorer nations too often having not accepted their social responsibilities.

Secondly, in *Centesimus annus* he responded not to the end of history, but to the end of the illusion that we can build a perfect social system: we will not get one here on earth and attempts to do so crucify man made in God's image as did national socialism and the Marxist variety. We must harmonise self-interest and the common good, otherwise bureaucracy stifles freedom, which is man's birthright.

Thirdly, while stressing that the morally operating free or market economy best serves the common good, he stresses that the Western capitalist variety is seriously defective. Under it, not all have access to the market. Making goods an end in themselves is an evil corrupting the physical and human environment. There has to be state action according to the principle of subsidiarity to assist those suffering poverty to recover from it and become independent again. But a social assistance state is not the answer. Democracy becomes totalitarian if it is not based on objective moral values. Without these, capitalist democracies become cultures of death - of contraception, abortion and euthanasia, as *Veritatis splendor* and *Evangelium vitae* show.

His life experience has included struggles with poverty and against Nazism and Communism and these gave him the soundest credentials in developing the social teaching of the Church, while his wide and profound learning uniquely enabled him to do so with consummate skill. A pontificate with so many triumphs for Christ and his Church has none greater than this. One of her greatest treasures, and surely the most neglected until now, is at last fully at her service. It is up to the experts in this field now to make sure it is.

MAKING SURE THAT WE PUT HIS ACHIEVEMENTS IN THIS AT THE SERVICE OF OUR PEOPLE

This teaching has, until now, been neglected for many reasons, the most important being that it has been taught very badly. This is mainly because as an academic subject, it lacks the methodology and syllabus that define other academic subjects. Specific contents of, for example, a theology, history, or other degree, will vary but each will have a serious literature on which to draw in working out a methodology and syllabus, so that the specific differences of varied approaches will be within the limits of what defines each as a subject. But there is no agreement among those who teach Catholic social doctrine about what it is, so that the serious academic discourse that leads to the formation of a serious literature cannot take place. Each expert creates his or her own version of it and rarely if ever do these versions meet. Hence serious teaching in this field cannot be done. The result is intellectual chaos.

The reason for this chaos is that while social doctrine is part of the Church's moral theological magisterium, from which it draws its principles, and draws heavily on the natural law concept and its implications, it is unlike any other sub-discipline in theology and Christian philosophy. The difference lies in the fact that those principles, and their application, can only be properly understood and applied by those who have a natural intellectual affinity with, and feeling for, the social sciences and in particular with the social and historical development of those societies and cultures in which Christian communities have lived over the centuries. They must be well-qualified in some aspect of the social and historical sciences to show how the principles they teach, have relevance to the real world.

Unfortunately, most of those the Church relies on to teach the subject are first and last theologians or philosophers, used to thinking in terms of absolutes, or theorising in the abstract. This cast of mind does not incline those who possess it to grappling with more practical matters, unless it be in personal terms. So in ethics, the personal is of concern: those areas of my life in which personal moral choice is at issue (e.g. to steal or not to steal). It is harder to deal with moralities of complex social, political and economic life unless you have learned to look at them through the eyes of the men and women who have to deal with them in practice. Here, past experience, usually of others is the only guide. Readiness to master the facts of that experience is required in order to interpret abstract principle.

Secondly, in understanding what social teaching within the Christian ethical and moral tradition has to say to us, we must be prepared to understand that teaching as the tradition understands it, and not through the prejudices of our own personal, political or social group. I came to realise this as I taught the subject at undergraduate and postgraduate level in London, Oxford and San Francisco from 1971-89. I had also published several books on it and its application, but came to realise that neither I nor any other specialist in the field that I knew of, had asked themselves what the teaching Church considered her social teaching to be. We blithely believed we were teaching it, but we were not. We were teaching our own versions of it. We needed to find out what the teaching Church thought on the matter. I decided I would not teach the subject again until I had had found out what that was.

Perhaps the Church had not cleared her mind on the subject. After all it was not for her to find the answer to the complex problems of society. This was for the theoretical experts in the various fields, thinkers and writers, and for the men of affairs, the practical men, the statesmen, the politicians, economists, businessmen, labour leaders, the people at the sharp end who had to make practical decisions. Natural law would guide the non-Christians; natural law and Christian ethics the latter. The Church's job was to help them discern where theories and practice did or did not measure up to natural law or Christian ethical standards, but she could only do that when the practical people and the social theorists were satisfied that they had come to terms with the issues and were considering alternative policies.

Fortunately by the end of the 1980's, with the confusion over the basis of personal morality, the disputes over liberation theology, the gradual disintegration of Soviet Communism and the sinister reappearance of liberal capitalism's advocates, the issues were clearing. That was one plus I could count on in my search. The other I found out as I proceeded with it. From the late 1970s, that clear-sighted philosopher and theologian John Paul II, and his equally clear-sighted, right-hand adviser on these matters, Cardinal Ratzinger, had these issues in their sights. And they faced up to them - personal morality in *Veritatis splendor* and *Evangelium vitae* and social morality in John Paul's *Laborem exercens* (1991) (3), *Solicitudo rei socialis* (1987) (1 and 41), and the Congregation for the Doctrine of the Faith's *Libertatis conscientia* (1986) (72 and 74): these tell us how the Church understands her personal, moral teaching and the social teaching which grows on it and out of it.

It is first of all scriptural; it uses the Bible's Old and New Testament understanding of man, his personal moral life and his social, moral life in civil, political and economic society. Secondly, it is theological. It is part of the Church's moral theological teaching, developed by her theologians from the scriptures, through Councils and popes, from the Fathers of the Church since the first century, down to the modern popes and the modern Church. Thirdly, it is historical. It has developed as the Church has responded to the problems of her people in social living, in different cultural, social, political and economic situations over the centuries. And finally, it is philosophical. It accepts the right reason, the natural insights of thinkers and activists in different cultures, Christian and non-Christian, on social ethics.

This framework, it seemed to me, provided a methodology, a strategy, a manner of studying the social teaching of the Church, which would reveal its wisdom and relevance. Note that while the modern social teaching is crucial, it is the last stage in its development. And unless that development is understood, it is difficult to teach the subject or guide others in its application. With that methodology, that strategy, I could then work out the tactics, the syllabus for teaching it to others to give them confidence in its wisdom and relevance.

This methodology enabled me to plan, research, write and get published over eight years, 1990-8, *Christian Social Witness and Teaching: the Catholic Tradition from Genesis to Centesimus annus*, two volumes, each of some 490 pages (Gracewing, 1998); and the chapters of those two volumes provide a syllabus for a one-year postgraduate MA in Catholic Social Doctrine. The profile of such a degree (some 3,500 words) has been accepted by two major English universities as being up to the academic standards required for such a degree.

With such a course established, the centre of academic excellence in the teaching of the subject can be developed and as it graduates students, their teaching, research, publications, and practical work will build up the expertise needed to serve the needs of the Catholic community in its social witness. I have been working on getting such an MA established for several years now and I have hopes of doing it.

Chesterton warned us in 1926, that 'the next great heresy is going to be an attack on morality, and especially on sexual morality, and it is coming from the living, exultant energy of the rich: the madness of tomorrow is not in Moscow but in Manhattan'. We now are witnessing the fulfilment of this prophecy. Morality is both personal and social and the two can never be separated. The second is built on the first; they are complementary and both must be thoroughly understood. It is a very serious intellectual challenge, and since the earliest times the Church has realised that its faith needs to be presented with all the powers of human reason and learning, as well as practised with all the fervour of hearts possessed by the love of God, if its mission is to succeed. We, as Catholic Christians in the modern world, have not until now met the intellectual challenge presented to us by this new heresy. We will not, unless we take seriously the moral teaching of the Church, personal and social, which John Paul II has brought to maturity. Only if we do, can we educate our Catholic people for life, for meeting the challenge of the Our Father in which we pray that his will be done 'on earth as it is in heaven'.

With young men and women graduates who have completed a postgraduate degree course for an MA in Catholic Social Doctrine, we could provide teachers from secondary school to postgraduate level who would thoroughly understand how the Church understands its social teaching. They could form a growing cadre of men and women, who would have an expert knowledge of the whole corpus of the documents I have discussed, and who would understand (a) a teaching based on three thousand years of experience of human society, back to the Old Testament times and (b) the social, political and economic situations to which the modern social documents of the Church were responses. Once we have a few score of such skilled teachers, and other graduates of the course who are in research, writing, or working in the social apostolate in some way, we can build up the publications, consultancy and other services to the Catholic community in this field.

IX

PASTOR AND DOCTOR:
THE ENCYCLICALS OF JOHN PAUL II

Aidan Nichols OP

This has been a very orderly pontificate. From the outset of his papal ministry, John Paul II was quite clear about which particular truths he wished to convey, what issues he wanted to address. And he proceeded to do so, systematically. Thus his first encyclical, *Redemptor hominis* (1979), sets out an entire programme for dealing with the doctrinal and spiritual weaknesses of contemporary Catholicism, as well as the wounds of the secular world, and, by implication, pledges the Pope to do what he can about them. In John Paul's mind, matters serious enough in themselves were given added urgency by the approach of the 'Great Jubilee', the opening of the new millennium in the year 2000. That was - from the beginning - the horizon he had in view *(cf. Redemptor hominis, 1)*.

Christ the centre

In the first words of his first encyclical, words often cited by his more acute interpreters since, John Paul II set his face against any humanistic or secularising interpretation of the texts and achievements of the Second Vatican Council: 'The redeemer of man, Jesus Christ, is the centre of the universe and of history.' Any notion that, at that Council, the Church had accepted a naturalism, albeit with a religious tincture, whereby in the future she would 'let the world set the agenda', and follow along as best she might, was at once scotched by that ringing declaration of the Christ-centredness of all reality.

That did not mean, of course, that the Pope denied the need for a response by the Church to society's ills. A religion of salvation, such as Catholic Christianity is, would have no *raison d'être* without diseases to cure. Nor did it mean that he abandoned the attempt to discern, in this context, the 'signs of the times' - the way Providence can draw attention, as the course of history unfolds, to peculiarly pressing needs of the world beyond the Church. In *Redemptor hominis* the Pope referred to such preoccupations of secular commentators as: inauthentic and illusory versions of freedom; the alienated character of much human work; technology's threat to the natural environment; lack of respect for human rights; exaggerated nationalism; consumerism, and 'slavery' to economic systems at large, as well as totalitarianism with its indifference to the common good.

But notice how these themes - as well as the more specifically 'Churchly' concerns (in order of appearance: collegiality, ecumenism, the current state of theology, the crises in Eucharistic sensibility and the practice of the sacrament of penance, marriage and celibacy) are all set within a Christological and ultimately, indeed, a Trinitarian perspective. For 'the mystery of Christ' constitutes 'the basis of the Church's mission and of Christianity' (11), and the

Christ in question is not the wandering prophet of exegetical scepticism. He is, rather, the 'Son of the living God' who 'became our reconciliation with the Father' (9). Nor is the Holy Spirit forgotten. In a beautiful (but densely written) passage, John Paul offered a commentary on the Pentecost Sequence (the well known Latin hymn, the *Veni Creator*).

> This invocation addressed to the Spirit to obtain the Spirit is really a constant self-insertion into the full magnitude of the mystery of the Redemption, in which Christ, united with the Father and with each man, continually communicates to us the Spirit who places within us the sentiments of the Son and directs us towards the Father. (18)

The Pope's subsequent encyclicals on the Father (*Dives in misericordia*, 1980) and the Holy Spirit (*Dominum et vivificantem*, 1986) would unpack these words by placing Christology in the context of the entire Holy Trinity.

But before launching into this Trinitarian catechesis, he wished to set down a marker. Against the backdrop of the humanistic 'horizontalism' of Catholic progressives in the 1970s, he affirmed that the divine dimension of the Redemption is what really shapes its human aspects. Unless we assimilate as thoroughly as possible the truths of the Incarnation and Atonement, no Christian account of how human beings are meant to live will be forthcoming. In a sense, it is extraordinary that a pope should feel it necessary to make so basic a point to the members of a dogmatic and supernaturalist Church. It is an index of how far things had degenerated in substantial areas of Western Catholicism by the end of Paul VI's pontificate, that John Paul II should consider that needed doing.

The whole Trinity

What do the other Trinitarian encyclicals of the Pope add? *Redemptor hominis* had stressed that, in Christ, man's true nature is divinely disclosed. A pope who in many ways exemplified the Renaissance ideal of the 'universal man' - the complete all-rounder - had declared his humanism to be theological through and through. Yet it could still be regarded as a cue for a false anthropocentrism. *Dives in misericordia* sets the record straight, accordingly, by treating Christ as, even more importantly, the revealer of the Father's face.

> The more the Church's mission is centred upon man - the more it is, so to speak, anthropocentric - the more it must be confirmed and actualised theocentrically, i.e. be directed with Jesus Christ to the Father. (*Dives in misericordia*, 1).

It is God, the Father, who is the supreme 'centre' for man: he sends the Son and the Spirit to bring us back to the truth of our own creation; yes - but even that is only a staging-post *en route* to our real destination, the Father's heart. The parable of the Prodigal Son - or, if one prefers, the Merciful Father, played a crucial role in the Pope's exposition here, and it is perhaps from the promulgation of this encyclical that one can date the extraordinary emergence of depictions of that text by Rembrandt (a Dutch Protestant) as a favourite Catholic icon. If Israel already knew a God who was rich in mercy - and the Pope defined mercy as 'a special power of love which prevails over the sin and infidelity of the chosen people' (*Dives in misericordia*, 4) - it is in the New Testament, with the teaching of Jesus and, above all, his Cross and Resurrection, that divine mercy shows how love is superior to justice. The Father's mercy is redemptive, restoring value to people, not simply condemning evil but drawing good from it. Here was a major source for John Paul II's criticism of much liberation theology as insufficiently reconciliatory. Still, to this extent the liberation theologians were right: the evils of the world will be met not by academic debate in a seminar on ethics, but by that kind of conversion to the Father which brings forth fruit in holiness of life. The more a secularised world distances itself from 'the Mystery of Mercy' (the Pope's name, in effect, for the Father), the more earnestly the Church has to invoke mercy on all. Interceding for people is not just liturgical good manners at the bidding prayers; it is or can be, as the great intercessory saints have known, the shedding of the heart's blood. In *Dominum et vivificantem*, the Pope shifted his focus from Father to Spirit. To the Pope's mind it was vital for the reinvigoration of the Church that Catholics should wake up to the presence of the Holy Spirit, since he is...

> ...the one in whom the inscrutable Triune God communicates himself to human beings, constituting in them the source of eternal life (1).

In a world too often spiritually arid, the Pope summoned back the faithful to that 'water welling up to eternal life' of which St John's Gospel had spoken (*Jn* 4:14). What the Pope tried to get people to see was that they had at their disposal supernatural resources - if only they would make use of them. Drawing on a centuries-long tradition of thinking about the Holy Spirit in the Latin church, John Paul II called him the 'uncreated Love-Gift' who enables human creatures to participate in the very life of God. But that was not only a summons to recognise how amazing our Christian dignity is. It was also a reminder to busy people who think they have to (as we say) 'make good' that, ultimately, all is gift. From the Holy Spirit,

> derives as from its source all giving of gifts *vis-à-vis* creatures...: the gift of existence to all things through creation; the gift of grace to human beings through the whole economy of salvation. (10)

None of this is said, be it noted, in the manner of charismatic euphoria. The 'price' of the Spirit's coming on the Church at Pentecost, in John Paul's exegesis of the Fourth Gospel, is the death of the Son who gives his disciples the Spirit 'through the wounds of his Crucifixion'. Catholic Christians must be enthused, the Pope was saying, but at a level deep enough to cost, for the way of the faith is a road of redemptive suffering.

The Mother of the Lord

In all three Trinitarian encyclicals there is a great deal of dogmatic meat, but above all in this last of the trio, on the Spirit. Not to be disconnected from the outreach to us of the Triune God is the Blessed Virgin Mary. In his encyclical on the Virgin, *Redemptoris mater* (1987), the Pope treated her as the woman who was made mother of all the supernaturally alive, by the actions of the Trinity itself. This is an encyclical which, like much of the Pope's strictly dogmatic writing, breathes the assurance of the Greek and

Latin Fathers when speaking of the principal mysteries of faith, and uses, often, their terms. Yet there were also some emphases of his own, sometimes with a view to capturing wider sympathies. We can note, for instance, how he speaks of Mary's gracing by God as, after Jesus himself, the pre-eminent example of divine election (and election is a theme central to much Reformation theology). Then there is the discreet appeal for the sympathy of the Orthodox East in the Pope's choice of references to commend his account of the Immaculate Conception: exclusively from Byzantine sources!

More indebted to the best contemporary Catholic theology (the influence of Hans Urs von Balthasar is surely detectable) is the Pope's statement that the kenotic character of Mary's faith - its obedience to the Word of God - united her to the Son's self-emptying on Calvary. But most notably, John Paul attempted a *capitatio benevolentiae* for his high Mariology *vis-à-vis* Western Catholics of a less traditionally devout kind, by presenting his doctrine as key to the notion (much favoured by 'progressive' believers) of the Church as the pilgrim people of God. Mary too made her pilgrimage of faith, and when she is preached and venerated she beckons others to follow her to the sacrifice of the Son and the love of the Father. The Pope spoke of Mary's faith as continually 'becoming' that of the pilgrim Church, passing over into that faith, and giving it its character as an unfinished project, an unbroken outreach. Finally, John Paul incorporated into his Marian synthesis a feature of liberationist writing about the Mother of the Lord: her *Magnificat* with its 'revolutionary' rhetoric shows that the truth about the God who saves cannot be separated from 'the manifestation of his love of preference for the poor and humble'. (37)

The mission of the Church

So marvellous a Gospel must needs be spread, and in the similarly entitled *Redemptoris missio* (1990), the Pope turned his attention to a sadly neglected topic - the foundations of mission, and the need to revivify a sense of the missionary imperative at a time when, in many quarters, the very phrase would be found politically incorrect. To those who maintained that missionary work was now excluded by dint of respect for the religious freedom of others, or rendered otiose by acknowledgement that any religion could be a way of salvation, John Paul replied that 'human development' and inter-faith dialogue, though in themselves admirable were also by themselves not enough. As much as any Evangelical, and for the same reason (it is the plain testimony of Scripture), the Pope confessed Christ as the only Mediator: 'the only one able to reveal God and lead to God'. There are no parallel or complementary mediators, but only agents who share Christ's mediatorial activity in such a way that everything they do takes its significance and value from what he is and does. Jesus Christ alone is the definitive self-revelation of God which is why the Church is 'missionary by her very nature' (5). John Paul II refused to countenance any division between the saving work of the divine Word in relation to human beings and the saving mission of Jesus - (some protagonists of inter-religious dialogue had been recommending dissevering the two so as to downplay the call to evangelise non-Christians). Jesus Christ is the indivisible God-man, the Word made flesh, centre and goal of history. Thus, the other world religions play a providential role only inasmuch as they either prepare for the Gospel or (in the case of post-Incarnation faiths) retain elements of it. This enables them to embody truths and virtues which compel respect - but it also leaves the missionary imperative intact. Here, in the Incarnate, Crucified and Risen Lord is a novelty which never grows old, and which nothing else can replace.

We can hope that millions who are non-Christians will be saved, and even that all will be saved, but if they are it will be in virtue of some tacit relation to Christ and his Church - where the full resources of supernatural goodness are alone made available, if only we will profit by them. On the Pope's reading of the Acts of the Apostles, the Church is:

> the house which all may enter and in which all can feel at home, while keeping their own culture and traditions, provided that these are not contrary to the Gospel. (24)

The Church is not UNESCO. She values cultures when they mediate truth, goodness, beauty. But her mission is to be their converter, not their curator. Saints Cyril and Methodius, the apostles of the Slavs, exemplified what was involved, as the Pope's own *Slavorum apostoli* (1985) suggested.

Church and society

What does the Pope have to say about the social teaching of the Catholic Church? In *Centesimus annus* (1991), John Paul II looked back at Leo XIII's *Rerum novarum* of just one hundred years before. The general principles Pope Leo had laid down had proved fruitful as a statement of what should transpire when the Church's ethos engages with modern society. John Paul II re-affirmed and further refined those principles. He emulated Leo XIII by looking around at the *nova* - the new developments or trends - of the late twentieth century as well as looking ahead to the next century: indeed the next millennium. (Here, as the Pope had to concede, his analyses could only be provisional, his prescriptions prudential). By a nice twist, John Paul II linked the much admired *Rerum novarum* to a less appreciated letter of Pope Leo's, *Libertas praestantissimum*, a text which had deplored the diffusion of intellectual and moral errors in the modern 'advanced' world. The social evils attacked in *Rerum novarum* were precisely the consequence of glorifying freedom - the freedom of economic and social innovation - without due regard, John Paul II explained, for the 'truth about man' (*Centesimus annus*, 4). The Church has to have a social message if she is to address the whole human being in his or her context. But equally, apart from the Gospel, no solution to the 'social question', as the nineteenth century called it, can be found. In this regard, the Pope is doing no more than being consistent with his own statement of 'Christ is the answer' in *Redemptor hominis*. What John Paul does in *Centesimus annus*, setting forth more compendiously themes already broached in *Laborem exercens* (1981) and *Sollicitudo rei socialis* (1987), is to take further the anthropological analysis in the Leonine letter, notably by developing its latent personalism. A man's labour gives him rights, but only a mind-set totally dominated by economics would think there is no more to the worker than his work. Over and above what is due to the employee, there are rights which 'flow from his essential dignity as a person' (*Centesimus annus*, 11). 'Real Socialism' - the Pope's sobriquet for Marxism-Leninism - is an anthropological non-starter. It cancels out the individual's subjectivity, subordinating him or her to the functioning of a socio-economic mechanism. And it ignores all those intermediary levels of life with others which have their own irreplaceable way of contributing to the common good. Not that the Pope's evaluation of consumer capitalism was any more flattering. The definition of man as 'a partially furred biped that shops' was unlikely to appeal to him. The fear haunting the later years of his pontificate has been that political democracy, so attractive when seen from behind curtains iron or bamboo, and with real merits, indeed, as an instrument of freedom, would ally itself with economic libertarianism and ethical relativism. In the democracies, freedom looked set to part company with truth.

Church and ethics

This was the theme of the Pope's encyclical on fundamental morals, *Veritatis splendor* (1993). Here John Paul laid down a mighty challenge to the common presumption of liberal society that freedom means arbitary choice - as well as switching on a warning light to moral theologians inclined to loosen the connections between ethical effort and the objectively right order of the world. For this Pope, freedom always needs shaping. It is when it is educated that it is liberated, and it is properly taught when it is taught by truth.

The 'splendour of truth' shines out above all in the Father's image, Jesus Christ, but for the good pagan, and for the Christian *qua* human being, it is already radiating in the work of creation and the moral reason of man. The Pope set his face against moral minimalism, holding that the moral life cannot be understood save in the context of the spiritual life. Thus even the ten commandments, all important inasmuch as they set, negatively, a limit beneath which none of us must ever fall, are only signposts for those setting forth on a journey.

If we are made in God's image and likeness then we shall truly be ourselves when our moral thinking shares in the divine wisdom - rather than claiming, falsely, to make up our own values by dint of human creativity as we go along. That espousal of 'participated theonomy' not over against human autonomy, but for the sake of our real (rather than counterfeit) flourishing, explains why the Pope could bring this encyclical to its climax by a eulogy of the saints. 'The life of holiness', wrote John Paul:

> which is resplendent in so many members of the People of God, humble and often unseen, constitutes the simplest and most attractive way to perceive at once the beauty of truth, the liberating force of God's love, and the value of unconditional fidelity to all the demands of the Lord's law, even in the most difficult situations. (107)

It was some of those 'difficult situations', where faithful Catholics accept hard tasks - natural sterility or the nurture of additional children, caring for the chronically ill or dying with dignity a natural death - that the Pope addressed in *Evangelium vitae* (1995). There, he pointed

out how invoking the medical profession to short-cut these
sacrificial demands of human living - by prescribing
artificial death, or the severing of new life from conjugal
love - can only seem appropriate to those already
immersed in what he termed, in a phrase with a future, a
'culture of death'.

Faith and reason

Behind much resistance to evangelical truth and Catholic
teaching there lay - so this Pope-philosopher was
convinced - bad metaphysics, or the yawning gap that
resulted from having no metaphysics at all. *Fides et ratio*
(1998), a real classic of Catholic Christian thinking, opens
by noting the undiminished vigour of the really basic
questions, such as: Who am I? Where have I come from?
Where am I going? Indeed, a culture where such questions
ceased to be put could barely be called human. Here the
Pope saw two roles for the Church; she tries to fathom
these deep questions in solidarity with a host of other
people on this planet, 'accompanying' them on their
search for truth. But she is also a witness to truths she
already knows under grace - she is a bearer of certitudes
and not just a poser of questions. That is why she does not
just agonise, but guides.

Philosophy, says the Pope, is one of the noblest of
human tasks - testifying to our ability to wonder, speculate
and construct systems of thought. From pondering the
history of philosophy, and the way people think the world
over, we can reach the conclusion that there is a core of
philosophical insight which constitutes a real spiritual
heritage for humanity. This is 'right reason': *orthodoxos*

logos the Greeks called it, and the Romans *recta ratio*, with aspects logical, ethical, aesthetic. Why should we care about it? Because it is needed as a foundation for any life, personal or corporate, worth the name. Otherwise all we are left with is a sink of relativistic scepticism. Philosophers, then, have a high vocation and a heavy responsibility for guiding thought, and with thought, culture as well.

So the Pope appealed for a renewal of metaphysics, remaking contact with that perennial heritage of basic truths and values. He recalled philosophy to its ancient sapiential function. Philosophy must be allowed its 'genuinely metaphysical range', its capacity to attain to what is 'absolute, ultimate, foundational' in its search for truth - not least for the sake of ethics, since the moral good has its ultimate foundation in the Supreme Good which is God. Our world may be anthropocentric but it should not be 'monothropic', only concerned with the human - for then it will miss out on the human, actually:

> It is metaphysics which makes it possible to ground the concept of their [human beings'] spiritual nature... The person constitutes a privileged locus for the encounter with being, and hence with metaphysical enquiry.

And the Pope did as his title promised, relating faith to reason, when he added:

> A theology without a metaphysical horizon could not move beyond an analysis of religious experience, nor would it allow the *intellectus fidei* [the understanding of faith] to give a coherent account of the universal, the transcendent value of revealed truth. (83).

However gently expressed, what an indictment of much a-metaphysical modern theology lay in those words! In an increasingly fragmented culture, what is known can seem too complex and insufficiently inter-related to be more than a maelstrom of facts in which the white water rafter soon goes under. John Paul II called for an end to further segmentation, and a new start on a 'unified and organic vision' - building on the best of earlier philosophy, both ancient and modern. That is not to say the Pope believed one could usefully pour everything that has been thought into a great vat of intellectual soup. He specifically warned against, for instance, eclecticism, historicism, scientism, pragmatism and nihilism, as dead ends for reflection. It was altogether typical of John Paul II that he should end this letter on faith and reason with an appeal to Catholic thinkers to 'philosophise in Mary', following the cue of a Byzantine monastic text which speaks, movingly, of the Mother of God as 'the table at which faith sits in thought'.

The reunion of believers

A Pope who reiterated so many distinctively Catholic emphases would not, one might think, be a good ecumenist. That judgement would itself be a mistake. For, first, John Paul II wove his specifically Catholic insights into a common Christian cloth. Even in my brief summary of these encyclical letters it must surely appear how much belongs with the shared Christian patrimony. But secondly, to be a Catholic Christian at all is to hold that the distinctively Catholic tenets are aspects of Christian fullness on whose absence other Christians are not so much to be congratulated as commiserated. As the Second

Vatican Council made clear, Catholic ecumenism can never be content with less than the whole truth.

Contrary to a widespread impression, assiduously cultivated at times by the radical sector of the Catholic press, John Paul II has devoted a huge amount of time and energy to that issue of 'divided Christendom'. *Ut unum sint* (1995) recognised that, thanks to the persistence of the baptismal covenant among Christians of all kinds, there is already a communion of a limited or imperfect kind between Catholics and others. Outside the visible unity of the Church are 'elements' of her life, free floating on the baptismal waters, and constituting means of salvation and sources of grace for separated believers. Rehearsing the principles which should guide authentic ecumenism and reviewing the fruits of the ecumenical dialogue (especially with the Eastern Churches where lies the greatest hope for reunion, if also at times the worst slings and arrows of verbal abuse), the Pope asked for the counsel and assistance of other Churches in the pursuance of his own task. In a way unheard of, even in the days of 'Good Pope John', he enlisted their aid in a redefinition of his office that it might better serve the two related aims of a supreme pastor: perfect unity in legitimate diversity.

Of course, so humble a plea was also, implicitly, a confident assertion of John Paul's faith (and that of the Catholic Church at large) that God in Christ has set in the midst of his people '...a ministry which presides in truth and love so that the ship [of the Church]... will not be buffeted by the storms and will one day reach its haven'. (97).

Eucharistic conclusion

The goal of ecumenism, and indeed of all Christian effort worth the name, can only be common participation in the Eucharistic banquet, which is for the Church the anticipation on earth of the life of the Kingdom. In *Ecclesia de eucharistia* (2003), his latest and, perhaps, last encyclical, Pope John Paul II had three aims in view. He wanted to offer an ordered account of Eucharistic doctrine, giving pride of place to the (recently neglected) truth that the Mass is the Holy Sacrifice, the accepted oblation of Easter in a sacramental sign. Secondly, he wished to underline the connexion of the Eucharist with the mystery of the Church. The foundations of the Church, both as new Israel and as sacred hierarchy, were laid when Christ made Covenant eucharistically, in the Upper Room. And so the Eucharist must be performed according to the apostolic rule of faith, it must be celebrated by the apostolic priesthood, in an unbroken succession of ministerial order. Except in special circumstances, the Church does not offer holy communion to non-Catholics because it is not one among many of ecumenism's strategies. Rather, it is the hoped-for crown of ecumenical endeavour. Finally, the Pope wanted to re-awaken in his readers a sense of wonder at the infinite dimensions of the Eucharistic mystery. Always to be carried out with the maximum dignity the liturgical actors can muster, nothing can be accounted too costly to do it honour. Beautifully, the Pope compares the work of Catholic artists and craftsmen, architects and musicians, to Mary, the sister of Lazarus, pouring precious ointment over the Saviour.

How does the Pope end? As a Dominican I am glad to see he does so by quoting the *Lauda Sion*, St Thomas Aquinas's great Eucharistic hymn. We have to re-learn our Eucharistic piety, says John Paul, 'at the school of the saints'. The saint he chooses here was, he points out, 'an eminent theologian and an impassioned poet of Christ in the Eucharist'. The combination of theological power with lyricism in *Ecclesia de eucharistia* makes one think Karol Wojtyla must be rather in the same mould.

In the encylical's concluding words:

If, in the presence of this mystery, reason experiences its limits, the heart, enlightened by the grace of the Holy Spirit, clearly sees the response that is demanded, and bows low in adoration and unbounded love. (62)

John Paul II on the day of his election 16th October 1978.

The World Youth Day celebrations in Rome 2000, one of John Paul II's greatest innovations.

John Paul II with Mother Teresa whose beatification took place on the 25th anniversary of the Pope's pontificate.

John Paul II's visit to the wailing wall and the Yad Vashem Holocaust memorial in Israel in 2000.

The set of the 25 stamps showing symbolic images of Pope John Paul II to celebrate the 25th anniversary of his pontificate, issued by Vatican Post on 20th March.